MEMOIR OF ITALO SVEVO

LIVIA VENEZIANI SVEVO

MEMOIR OF ITALO SVEVO

TRANSLATED BY ISABEL QUIGLY
PREFACE BY P. N. FURBANK

THE MARLBORO PRESS
MARLBORO, VERMONT

First American edition.

This English translation first published 1989.

Originally published in Italian under the title
Vita di Mio Marito
by Edizioni dello Zibaldone, Trieste, 1950.
Second, revised, edition, 1958.

The publication of the present volume has been
made possible by a grant from the National
Endowment for the Arts.

Manufactured in the United States of America

Library of Congress Catalog Card Number 89-63597

Cloth: ISBN 0-910395-57-8
Paper: ISBN 0-910395-58-6

CONTENTS

ACKNOWLEDGEMENTS

The letters and extracts from letters by James Joyce to Italo and Livia Svevo (translated from Joyce's original Italian, except for the letter written in English on pp. 135–6) are reproduced by kind permission of the Society of Authors as the literary representative of the Estate of James Joyce.

Stanislaus Joyce's translation of Svevo's lecture on James Joyce, in the Appendix, is used by kind permission of James Laughlin of New Directions.

PUBLISHER'S NOTE

This English translation has been made from the dall'Oglio edition of 1976. Some explanatory notes have been added, adapted mainly from the annotated edition by Anita Pittoni (Edizioni dello Zibaldone, Trieste, 1958). P. N. Furbank's *Italo Svevo: The Man and the Writer* (Secker and Warburg, 1966) and John Gatt-Rutter's *Italo Svevo: A Double Life* (Clarendon Press, 1988) were also consulted with much benefit.

Quotations from Italo Svevo have been printed in heavier type throughout to distinguish them from other quotations. Some passages from Svevo's letters or other writing in this volume appeared in English translation in P. N. Furbank's study. Where this occurs, Mr Furbank's existing translations have been used, with his permission. The publisher wishes further to thank P. N. Furbank for his valuable support of this project from the beginning.

At the end of her book, Livia Veneziani Svevo reproduced a selection of the letters of condolences she received after her husband's death. To avoid the repetitiveness of such material, this edition omits short letters from Valerio Jahier and Paul-Henri Michel.

Italo Svevo's lecture on James Joyce, given in Milan in 1927, has been added as an appendix. Stanislaus Joyce's original translation has been checked against the original Italian, and corrected where necessary, by John Gatt-Rutter.

It is excellent to have an English translation of the memoir of
Italo Svevo by his widow Livia Veneziani. It is a book full of
charm – not only the charm of that quite extraordinary
individual 'Italo Svevo' (otherwise Ettore Schmitz), but also
of Livia's own very attractive, serene, clear-cut and strong-
willed character. As she explains herself, she wrote the book
during the later years of the Second World War and in tragic
circumstances: two of her grandchildren had gone missing as
prisoners of war in Russia, and a third was killed during the
liberation of Trieste. That it should be such an inspiriting
and entertaining book is a tribute to her; but of course even
more so to Svevo himself, by whose comic genius Darwin-
ism, *fin-de-siècle* 'senility' and Schopenhauerian pessimism
are transformed into a marvellously invigorating view of life.

Italo Svevo is certainly a 'name', and *The Confessions of
Zeno* at least is usually in print; but even now I am inclined to
think that he is not read quite as widely as he should be. The
profundity of a comic genius is at a certain disadvantage as
against that of more straight-faced and conventionally
'serious' writers; and perhaps Proust, whose humour is as
profound as Svevo's, would not enjoy the popularity that he
does if his novel were predominantly in a comic mode. Not
indeed that *The Confessions of Zeno* (let alone *As a Man Grows
Older*) is a 'comic' novel in any simple sense; for part of the
strength of *Zeno* is its controlled transitions from wild farce to
the most severe and poignant Zolaesque 'realism'. Still, *As a
Man Grows Older* and those other lesser but brilliant works,
Short Sentimental Journey, 'The Hoax', 'The Nice Old Man
and the Pretty Girl', are all expressions of a similar vision,
which may properly be called 'comic', and by the help of

which anxieties about what constitutes 'health' – that bug-bear of turn-of-the-century thought – are put to rest in a quite unexpected fashion. In this vision 'illness' or the *mal-du-siècle* come to be seen as indistinguishable from life itself and are restored to the order of nature.

Livia Svevo's book records for us how those spiralling self-doubts and compulsions, and convictions of 'senility', which are explored with such ironic detachment and curiosity in the novels were, at the time of their courtship and marriage, all too real a phenomenon for Svevo and no joke at all. She did not pretend to understand them, and Svevo fairly soon gave up any ambition of explaining himself to her; on the other hand she reacted to them in a thoroughly salutary way. Svevo had mentally assigned her a definite role, and it was a role that, whether or not it represented her true nature, she was willing and well-equipped to play. She was 'my blonde, my sole and great, great hope of true, solid happiness'; she was to be the fixed point that his life could make its eccentric circles around. 'Even after a year [of marriage] my wife takes everything seriously' writes Svevo in his 'Family Chronicle' (see p. 38).

Her husband – good God! The father of her children! And all the other degrees of parentage too – all of them taken seriously! . . . She doesn't realize it, but I believe that in this regard she has not got as far as the French Revolution yet, and a *lettre de cachet* from patriarchal authority, counter-signed by the King, would not cause her much indignation. Think of it, the King! What an honour to be locked up by order of the King!

One of his favourite emotions or obsessions about her is posthumous jealousy. He always insisted that she must marry again after he was dead, and in an engaging little sketch entitled 'Livia' he pictures the whole scene of her remarriage. He has been dead for six months, and Livia and her mother agree that it is time she accepted her new suitor, a tall, handsome man with magnificent teeth and most un-*fin-de-siècle* moustaches. She tells the latter she has always been attracted to him – or if not *quite* at first, then only because she was already engaged. To her surprise he obviously believes her (Ettore, i.e. Svevo, would not have done so). Her mother leaves the room, and the suitor gives her a kiss (Ettore's ghost groans protestingly from the door-hinges). 'Your past belongs to you,' says the suitor, stroking his moustaches imposingly; 'but I want to be told about it, if you please.' She tells him about K.; he says nothing. She tells him about M., and he laughs. Finally she begins to tell him about Ettore himself, and at once he interrupts her. 'I'm not worried about *him*,' he says (the door screeches piteously). 'Your mother has already told me you only took him out of pity.' She stares at him, but doesn't protest, reflecting that it is all for the best. So poor Ettore has to die twice over.

We may thus take Livia's memoir as, emotionally speaking, a true account of Svevo and of their marriage. What needs to be pointed out, however, is that, from a factual point of view, Livia is in one respect deliberately misleading. There is no reference in her book to the very important fact of Svevo's Jewishness. Jews had a somewhat favoured status in Trieste, as compared with other parts of the Austro–Hungarian empire, and the Schmitzes, at least during their prosperity, were prominent figures in the local Jewish community. Svevo attended Jewish schools, both in Trieste and in Germany; and though he was personally hostile to all organized religion, Judaism included, considering it a vexatious nuisance, his Jewishness was a serious obstacle in his courtship of the *bien-pensant* and Catholic Livia. (She was herself quarter-Jewish, but it was a fact that she and her family were eager to forget.) Svevo stood by his secularist principles and, much against Livia's will, they were married by a civil ceremony. However, in 1897, having given birth to a daughter, Letizia, Livia fell seriously ill and began to brood on her sin in marrying a Jew. Upon this Svevo cheerfully offered to have himself baptized and went along to find a priest. Learning the catechism, however, proved beyond his powers; so at last he gave the priest an ultimatum: 'Either I get baptized without learning from memory, or I don't get baptized at all.' At this, the priest baptised him on his own terms; and when Livia was sufficiently recovered, they had a church wedding.

It was Svevo's wish, expressed in writing, that when he died he should be given a 'simple, modest, and *civil* funeral'. He wanted, he said, to be as little nuisance to his fellow-citizens as possible and for things to be straightforward, 'without ostentation of any kind, *even of simplicity*'. Livia obeyed his instructions, and he was buried in the Israelite cemetery in Trieste. However, a year or two later, she had him exhumed and reinterred in the Veneziani family tomb in the Catholic cemetery of Sant'Anna. A family acquaintance, the writer and editor Anita Pittoni, recalled Livia's phlegmatic comment: 'Ugh! He was all covered with horrible brown specks.' Eventually Livia herself suffered over the Jewish issue. During the early days of the Second World War she was told she must ratify her racial status with the 'Race Office'. She went to Rome to do this and spent weeks there trying to register herself as an Aryan – with no result, till eventually it was explained to her that what was necessary was a bribe, of fantastic proportions – whereupon in despair she declared herself a Jew. It put her in serious danger, and she had to flee from Trieste and take refuge in Treviso province, taking with her a huge trunk full of Svevo's manuscripts and letters. Her book was thus written in daily terror of the Nazis.

Livia became a devoted propagandist for Svevo's importance as a writer, as did her daughter Letizia. It was, however – as she relates – James Joyce who first promoted Svevo's international reputation. They had come into contact in Trieste in 1907, when Svevo engaged Joyce to coach him in English. Svevo had one day admitted to Joyce that he had been a writer, and he lent him his two novels, *Una Vita* and *Senilità*; and at the next lesson Joyce told him he was an unjustly neglected author and there were pages in *Senilità* which Anatole France could not have improved on. Indeed he could already repeat some paragraphs by heart. (It was Joyce who later gave Svevo a title, *As a Man Grows Older*, for the English translation.) Joyce's championship was an important factor in that resurrection, or 'miracle of Lazarus', of a writer who had not only been ignored but had in middle life deliberately renounced 'that ridiculous and damnable thing called literature' and only returned to it when the 1914–18 war left him without other occupation.

Joyce would endlessly question Svevo about Jewish life, and it seems he may have taken a detail or two from Svevo when creating Leopold Bloom. It was also, as Livia records, a favourite theme of Joyce's that he had borrowed Livia's name and magnificent hair 'to adorn the little river which runs through my city, the Anna Liffey'. She was not at all pleased when later she heard that, in his *Anna Livia Plurabelle*, two washerwomen were scrubbing dirty clothes in the Liffey.

Svevo chose the pseudonym 'Italo Svevo' ('Italus the Swabian') to express his feeling of being a hybrid, an Italian by language, an Austrian by citizenship and a German by ancestry and education. The feeling was of the greatest benefit to his art, but it may have been a slight handicap to his reputation. When in 1931 a bust of him was erected in the Public Gardens at Trieste, the official speeches made no reference to the Parisian critics, Valery Larbaud and Benjamin Crémieux, who were the real architects of his fame, nor was a telegram from Joyce read out. It has been Svevo's fate to suffer in this way from possessiveness, and attempts have been made to claim him for a variety of sectional interests – for Triestine regionalism, Italian irredentism, and 'eternal-Jewishness' – usually with an unspoken rebuke for not having shown more commitment. But equally he has suffered from a kind of disowning. For reasons deep in

xiv   cultural and linguistic history, the Italians for long felt rather
hung up about Svevo, with perhaps a touch of unconscious
resentment at having had him thrust upon them by foreign
critics; thus they have tended to harp rather obsessively on
something called the Svevo 'affair'. The paradox of such a
fate, to be both coveted and unwelcome, and in each case for
a wrong reason, is one that Svevo would have analysed with
zest. (Indeed it was rather what he felt about the age
problem; throughout his life, by some mischance – he said –
he had always seemed to be the wrong age.) None the less we
may regret it a little, for it helps to give the impression that he
is a 'coterie writer', whereas, quite as much as Kafka or
Proust, he is a writer for all the world.

P. N. FURBANK

MEMOIR OF ITALO SVEVO

MY MEMORIES OF ETTORE go back to my childhood, since we were distantly related: his mother, Allegra Moravia, was the sister of my grandfather, Giuseppe Moravia, who came from San Daniele in Friuli. But my memory of the Schmitz family home is more vivid after I left school, at Notre Dame de Sion in Trieste; it was of a patriarchal house, enlivened by eight high-spirited children. My earliest years and childhood had been spent partly in Marseilles and I had returned to Trieste in 1885, when I was eleven. I saw Ettore again in 1892 at his father's deathbed, where all the relations were gathered. The links of affection between us all were very strong. From that time I began to visit the family and to spend time with Ettore's sisters, Paola and Ortensia. Twice a week I would go to the large fine house in Corsia Stadion, where the Schmitzes had all remained, even after the financial ruin of their father, who had been an experienced and prosperous businessman. I used to give lessons in French, which I had studied at an elementary level, to little Sarah, the daughter of Paola who, after her divorce, acted as mother to the children; and I nearly always met Ettore finishing his lunch, having come home in the early hours of the afternoon from the Union Bank where he was employed. He was then a tall, thin young man, with raven-black hair, a fine, clear, velvety voice, plainly dressed and with a very lively manner. Together we talked a great deal – the kind of talk, naturally, which could take place between an eighteen-year-old girl just out of the convent and a man of thirty-one, who was experienced but respectful. I thought him very cultivated and regarded him with some awe, having discovered his literary past, which he never mentioned. That he was well known in Trieste as a literary critic writing in the *Indipendente*, an ardent irredentist[1] newspaper, I knew, and

1. Irredentists – from *Italia irredenta* (unredeemed Italy) – were those who took part in or supported the struggle to free predominantly Italian-speaking regions – like Venezia Giulia, of which Trieste was the main city – from Austrian rule and unite them with Italy.

that he was a close friend of Umberto Veruda, the defiant leader of bohemian life in Trieste, who used to amble along the Corso, flamboyantly dressed.

With me Ettore behaved sensitively and respectfully. He confided in me at once that he intended to give up smoking – an obsession throughout his life – because it was bad for the lungs. We even made a bet: if he did not smoke for three months, I would give him a kiss. When the three months were up, he demanded the prize for his strong-mindedness and kissed me on the cheek.

Next day I received the works of Manzoni, magnificently bound, inscribed:

To my cousin Livia, in memory of her good-heartedness, because, although it was unsuccessful, she wanted to help me in my struggle against vice; but also as a reminder of my deception, the better action of the two.

Trieste, 13.1.1895.

The truth was that he had secretly continued smoking, and his sisters Paola and Ortensia had helped to deceive me. On the day of our engagement he wrote under the earlier inscription: 'A kiss, once given, is never lost.'

Four years passed. Our friendship continued calmly and we did not think it was hiding the seed of a tenderer feeling. He used to come to our house, which was always hospitable; he attended our big Christmas dinner and, with Veruda, took part in the parties on Sunday afternoons.

It was a sad event which brought this tenderer feeling to light. In October 1895 Ettore's mother, a sweet, gentle woman whose features resembled his own, was dying. With the rest of the family I was in her room and, seeing Ettore so dejected, I offered him a glass of Marsala to give him a little strength. Later he confessed that this affectionate gesture had had a very special meaning for him. From that moment he began to think of me more intensely, with a warmer feeling; not as a dear young cousin, but as the woman he needed. After a few weeks, though usually so hesitant in making decisions, he spoke to my mother about it.

Olga Moravia Veneziani, my mother, was a woman of unusual energy, clear intelligence and remarkable business enterprise. The reins of the family were firmly in her hands and she took an active part in the management of the large firm dealing in marine paint which my father had founded. After the difficult years in Marseilles, they had become comfortably off. My father, although only an amateur chemist, had, after a long period of research discovered a process of making paint for the keels of ships. The new industry was continually advancing.

We were five children. My father's favourite was Bruno, the only boy; after him he favoured me, while my sisters Nella, Fausta and Dora counted a little less. My mother had dreamed of a brilliant marriage for me; Ettore's modest position as a mere clerk in the Union Bank, without any expectations from his family after his father's financial ruin, was therefore an obstacle to our union. She also disliked the difference in our ages – thirteen years – and although she was fond of Ettore, she strongly opposed the marriage, and with her usual energy told him he was not to speak to me about it. The secret was revealed to me instead by my cousin Bianca Veneziani. When I knew about Ettore's feelings, I too began thinking of him and when we met felt uneasy. He understood my state of mind and tried to see me when he could. I continued to visit his home, where his gentle sister Paolina had taken over from their mother, and there we spoke of our love. As soon as he was sure of my feelings, he spoke formally of marriage to my parents, and after some lively discussions managed to win through: we were engaged on 20 December 1895.

BEFORE SAYING ANYTHING about the years of our very happy union, I should like to go back to Ettore's childhood and early youth, putting my memories in order and looking through old papers. He told me about many episodes in those early years of his life, tender, funny, sad.

His was an old-fashioned family, with no less than sixteen children, of whom only eight survived into adult life: Paola, Natalia, Noemi, Adolfo, Ettore, Elio, Ortensia and Ottavio. Whenever a new child was born, the father, Francesco Schmitz, would exclaim: 'Today my capital has been increased by a million!' The four boys and four girls, who were all intelligent and full of life, grew up in great friendliness, and Ettore's childhood was happy and unruffled. His mother's sweetness tempered his father's strictness. She was called Allegra, and something of her name emanated from her, irradiating the atmosphere around her. Often she would stand at the window, watching her children go out together, like a row of organ pipes. But one of the pipes was often missing: Ettore would be trailing, absent-minded, mislaying things. The future man of letters, head in the clouds, was already visible in him. Full of intelligence and ideas, the small family group kept inventing new forms of amusement. They even established a handwritten newspaper, each part of it edited by one of the children. Family events were often recorded with very humorous comments, betraying the hand of Adolfo, who had a happy, playful temperament. The only copy preserved among the family papers, yellow with age, has the mysterious title 'Adotajejojade', a strange word formed from the initials of the children's nicknames.

When the Schmitz parents were planning a trip to Italy, the following comment appeared: 'Great discontent reigned at the news that with their majesties' departure the kingdom is to be placed under the regency of the archduchess Natalia . . .' (Natalia was the second sister). When the parents arrive in Naples, the weather forecast says: 'On the 17th, Prof. Palmieri in Vesuvius University will discover a new constellation in the sky of Naples, which will be called: The Schmitzes.' In the advertisements we read that Elio, who was tall and thin, 'is putting himself forward for a series of useful though modest jobs: roadsweeper, broomstick, giraffe'. Sensational news: 'A dog has been lost (fattish) answering to the name of Ettore. As he is rather lazy and likes sleeping in the sun, it will be easy to find him near the aqueduct. If he is found asleep, please do not wake him. Ettore, Ettore, a plump little dog.'

But this happy community was soon to be broken up. Ettore was twelve when, with Adolfo and Elio, he had to leave for boarding-school at Segnitz, near Würzburg. One evening at table he had mispronounced a German name absurdly and his father (who said that a good businessman in Trieste must know two languages) decided to send him to Germany to learn the language perfectly. Francesco Schmitz did not consider German his mother tongue. His father, Adolfo Schmitz, an official in the Austrian empire who came from the Rhineland, had married Rosa Macerata at Treviso, where his job had taken him. As the son of an Italian mother, Francesco considered himself Italian. His name often appeared amongst those of the most ardent patriots. Being good at business himself, he hoped to make his sons into good businessmen, and sent them to Germany purely to prepare them for what he thought the best of careers. For this reason he had chosen a school which was mainly commercial. In any case, this strict father's motto was 'Manly men are not made from boys brought up at home'.

Thus a new life began for the three boys in the distant region of Main in a foreign land, among foreign people. Elio, who was as thin as a reed, very tall for his age, very sensitive, and in love with music, could not stand up to the severe discipline of the school. Despite the encouragement of his brother Adolfo, who loved him tenderly and protected him, he had to go back after a few months to his beloved birthplace, to the warmth of home with his mother, sisters, and the two youngest who were still babies. Ettore, on the other hand, stood up to things very well. In a few months he had learned German and formed an intellectual group among the boys, as well as gaining the friendly encouragement of some of the masters with his lively intelligence. He and his schoolmates held discussions on philosophy. A sign of this early intellectual excitement remains in a short philosophical thesis written in German, in opposition to that of a fellow-pupil called Bratter. Ettore already had a great love of reading and learning. He read the German classics early, was enthusiastic about the novels of the humorist Friedrich Richter (Jean Paul), devoured those of Turgenev, and, in a fine translation, read Shakespeare, who fascinated him.

Ettore's adolescence consisted of long periods of intense study at school and short, delightful holidays at home, irradiated by the sun of Trieste and the joy of the sea. He was a good swimmer and loved sea bathing. Relations with his siblings were tender, and understanding and friendship increased as they grew up. Each developed his or her own gifts: Paola, the eldest sister, learned to paint from the artist Eugenio Scomparini; Ortensia specialized in singing, Natalia in the piano; Elio, destined to die young, loved music, and the passionate study of the violin both delighted and tormented him. Adolfo, who had a fiery temperament, dedicated himself to irredentist politics. Only Ottavio, who was enterprising and serious, seemed to have inherited his father's positive qualities. At the age of eighteen he settled in Vienna, starting on a brilliant career in banking. Ettore, on the other hand, always felt a strong literary vocation and spent sleepless nights reading.

In his diary Elio tried to relive his quiet adolescence and wrote of Ettore: 'He is using his savings to start a library.' And later: '. . . I can still see the only tidy things in our room on those bookshelves: Schiller, Goethe. When he had Shakespeare, he read all night and spent many sleepless nights bent over *Hamlet* . . .' Elsewhere he wrote: 'I was sorry to see him so enthusiastic about German literature that he neglected Italian literature, and told him to read a little

Dante and Petrarch, who were as good as the Germans. He laughed in my face and exclaimed: "Schiller is the greatest genius in the world."'

Elio was his brother's first biographer, the first to read his mind, to have faith in him, to examine him and stimulate him, to follow every literary effort he made. In his short life he was closer than anyone else to Ettore. 'No historian admired Napoleon as much as I admired Ettore,' Elio wrote in his diary, which Ettore preserved religiously for his whole life, like a precious relic.

When he was eighteen and had completed his studies, Ettore left school and Germany, and returned to Trieste to attend the Istituto Superiore Commerciale Revoltella,[1] though with little enthusiasm. With him he brought a favourable memory of the school's headmaster, a strict, austere but just man whose authority he had accepted with filial feelings. In his heart too, he kept the tender memory of an idyll: the image of the headmaster's niece, young Anna Herz, who had preferred him to his brother Adolfo. Sadly, this threw a shadow between the brothers, which Ettore never liked to recall. Anna was older than Ettore, and there was a touch of motherly protectiveness about her feelings, apparent in an inscription in the works of Shakespeare, presented to him when he left school.

In the new life Elio became his dearest, his only, friend. Ettore was becoming more and more attracted to literature and suffered from not being in perfect command of the Italian language, partly because he had been educated in a foreign school, and partly because of the constant use of dialect, spoken at home even by cultured families in Trieste. Secretly he had a dream of persuading his father to send him to study in Florence for a few years, to learn the language at its living source. But he knew that this was just a beautiful fantasy, and that it was his destiny to become a businessman

1. A commercial high school founded by Baron Pasquale Revoltella, a Triestine financier.

like his brother Adolfo. This had been settled by his father. Literature was a very long way from anything old Schmitz had in mind and, despite his ardent longing to be a writer, Ettore lacked the strength to oppose the will of his father, who ruled the family authoritatively and whose prosperity was declining. Ettore could not resist the force of circumstances and environment, though he continued to nourish a faint hope in his heart. The only person in whom he confided his disagreement, his only support, his only spur, was Elio. Despite obstacles, Ettore thought ceaselessly of writing. His literary efforts followed one another in a confused way, and his only judge was his faithful brother. 'Since the 10th of this month,' Elio wrote in his diary, 'Ettore has been writing a play in "martellian" verse:[1] *Ariosto Governatore* (*Ariosto the Governor*). So far he has written twenty verses. But he is rather slow in everything and I don't know when this, his first work, will be finished. So far he has never finished anything. This time, though, I made him sign a contract in which he promised me that by 14 March he would have finished *Ariosto Governatore*, otherwise he would pay me 10 soldi for every cigarette he smoked for the next three months.'

On the day before the contract expired, however, Elio was writing disappointedly: '3 March 1880. Today Ettore came to me and said: "I can't honour the contract I made with you. I'm not going to carry on the *Ariosto Governatore*, but I'm going to start another play which I've already got a subject for: *Il Primo Amore* (*First Love*). I don't want to be forced to write so quickly, though. Give me some extra time." So I made him sign five promissory notes to mature twenty days ahead, starting on the 14th, that is, tomorrow. He has three weeks to write each act.' But this contract was not honoured either, and Elio complained uneasily: '18 June 1880. Ettore has started a new play. He won't be finishing the last one.

1. i.e. alexandrines, named after Pier Jacopo Martello (1665–1727).

"Le Roi est mort; vive le Roi!" But I don't think he'll finish
this one, either.'

At that time the theatre completely absorbed Ettore. His first story was to come much later. The name of a very young actress often appears in Elio's diary, a wonder of the day, adored by audiences. Her name was Gemma Cuniberti. All the young in Trieste loved the theatre in those days: singers had the horses taken from their carriages and were pulled along by their admirers; actors were acclaimed as stars. Ettore had even longed to become an actor, and had practised a great deal to get over the way he pronounced his 'r's. However, harsh reality and bitter experience soon put paid to all his dreams and gave him a new direction in life. His father, who, to expand his business, had put all his capital into a large glass-making firm, collapsed financially. The blow aged him prematurely. The family was now nearly poor, their hospitable house no longer open for their delightful parties, the pretty sisters no longer able to expect large dowries. They could no longer take part in the elegant life of rich society in Trieste, with a box at the theatre and a carriage for the parade in the Boschetto. Ettore's father was never again to start up in business.

To help the family, Ettore had to interrupt his studies and get a job quickly in any firm he could find. Farewell forever to his dream of going to Florence! His heart was torn by the sight of his father's ruin and he now had to think of earning a living. In the depressed man his father had become he could no longer see the man he had admired so much for his strength, his rectitude, and his shrewdness in business.

However, Ettore's literary aspirations, though temporarily put aside through urgent necessity, irresistibly returned. Even during these upheavals he began a new play entitled *I Due Poeti* (*The Two Poets*). And when, having reached the age for military service, he had to take time off from his job to go to lessons in preparation for the exam as a 'volunteer' (obligatory for students in the Austrian empire), he was glad to be able to steal a few hours from these lessons in which to write his plays.

It was on a very important date that Elio wrote in his diary: '27 September 1880. Today Ettore went into the bank and liked it very much.' Now began Ettore's methodical life as a junior employee. He started working in the correspondence department of the Trieste branch of the Union Bank of Vienna, and stayed there for eighteen years. In these colourless surroundings he managed to find the atmosphere for his first novel, *Una Vita* (*A Life*), which dealt with the secret passions underlying an apparently uniform existence, and in which several characters from the middle-class business world of Trieste appear.

Outwardly Ettore seemed a diligent, punctual and conscientious employee, but parallel with this outer existence went a secret life in which his spirit was tormented and he examined himself. 'He seems apathetic,' Elio wrote, 'since the main part of his life is in his mind and in himself.' And so it was: the deepest part of his life was revealed very seldom, even to his family, but his longing for knowledge was not satisfied by his work. Despite strict orders from his father, he would stay up all night with his books.

All the odd moments, all his free time, were spent in study. Ettore felt that he lacked literary culture; he wanted to arrange his chaotic knowledge, to fill the gaps, above all to familiarize himself with the Italian literary tradition. His evening hours were spent in the quiet reading-room of the public library, which had all the classics. Machiavelli and Boccaccio alternated with Guicciardini. De Sanctis[1] was Ettore's guide, but he never really followed any method in his reading: he followed his own taste, and sometimes just a whim. He particularly admired Giosuè Carducci,[2] the hero of

1. Francesco de Sanctis, leading Italian literary historian and critic, who wrote an influential history of Italian literature, and was the champion of Émile Zola in Italy.
2. Giosuè Carducci, poet, critic and literary historian who expressed a strong Italian patriotism.

the irredentists, whereas he neglected Manzoni, and bitterly
regretted it later. But although these were the works he
decided to study, his tastes always led him to the nineteenth-
century narrative. He was always drawn to the novel, and
abandoned the German classics to concentrate on the French
naturalists. He devoured Flaubert and Daudet; Zola was his
god. He loved reading Balzac and spent a great deal of time
on Renan. These writers were the companions of his evenings and nights. By day he carried out his work as a
correspondence clerk diligently, getting on well with his
office colleagues whom he treated in a polite and friendly
way. Already, from the life at the bank, he was unconsciously
collecting material for a future novel. In his free time he filled
a great many notebooks, in surroundings peopled with his
own ghosts.

Trieste, where several races and various cultures meet,
provided a favourable setting for his development. French
and German novels were read in the original, the Russians in
various translations; there was also an interest in music and
painting. Ettore's temperament was eclectic; he loved every
form of art. He belonged to the Music Club for those who
loved classical music (he had started playing the violin as a
boy), and to the Artists' Club, which was the centre of a
group of heterogeneous painters: those who had come down
from the north, influenced by the theories of the Munich
school, clashed with the Latin ideas of the Venetian school.

The city's literary life was distinct from that of Italy, a self-
enclosed world with its own particular character, wholly
occupied with the memory of Roman and Venetian civilization, and with defending the national heritage. It centred on
the literary salon of the poet Elisa Tagliapietra-Cambon, in
the 'Minerva' study group then directed by her husband, the
lawyer Luigi Cambon, and the librarian and historian Attilio
Hortis, and in the editing of the daily *Indipendente*, the
standard-bearer of irredentism in Giulia. Its first editor was
Giuseppe Caprin, a brilliant recorder of the past; its second,

the combative journalist Riccardo Zampieri, friend of Oberdan;[1] and articles by the best writers in Trieste appeared in it. The learned Attilio Hortis, the poet Cesare Rossi, the romantic Riccardo Pitteri, the versatile young Silvio Benco, who was just starting out, all wrote passionate articles for the rebel paper, which the Austrian authorities banned on many occasions. But it not only flew the flag for the Italian cause; it also provided the only outlet for the literary young of the irredentist provinces. It was natural that Ettore should wish to contribute to it. His first article appeared on 2 December 1880. The faithful Elio's diary could not fail to mention such an important event: 'The night before, that is, the previous evening, because he'd written it in a few minutes, he showed me an article which he wanted to have published in the *Indipendente*, but he came back at nine to tell me he had taken it into the editor's office and had spoken to Caprin, who had accepted it, with a few cuts.'

The publication of this article began a loyal association between Ettore and the paper, which lasted for many years. In his articles he hid behind the pseudonym of E. Samigli, a name he later gave to the main character in the story 'Una Burla Riuscita' ('The Hoax'). He wrote critical studies, philosophical essays, general pieces. Poetry he did not care for. He once said to me: 'Why so many words for such few ideas?'

He was an enthusiastic admirer of Wagner, and the first person in Trieste to write about Wagner's aesthetic ideas in the newspaper. I still have a copy of the issue of 22 December 1884, with the article 'The Autobiography of Richard Wagner', expressing Ettore's admiration for the great composer who had died a few months earlier. I have other yellowing copies he kept, with his best articles: a review of *Il Libro di Don Chisciotte* by Edoardo Scarfoglio (8 September 1884) and 'The Truth about a Talk Given by Ernest Renan in

1. Guglielmo Oberdan, a Trieste student executed in 1882 for a plot against the life of the Austrian emperor, Franz Josef.

his Native City' (14 August 1884). They show the wide range of his interests and the cultural horizons towards which he was looking. However, it was to creative literary work that he most ardently aspired. Although his life seemed to follow a monotonous rhythm, his inner world was continually tormented. In the daytime, he had the bank; in the evenings, a walk along the Corso, the library, a pause at the café; at night, writing for the paper; interspersed with swimming in the sea or cycling to the highlands of the Carso[1] on Sundays.

Nothing is left to us, not even among his unpublished work, of these first attempts mentioned in Elio's diary. Elio continued to be the accurate recorder of his brother's plans and of what he wrote:

'4 January 1881: Ettore keeps writing without pause; as I now write he is beside me, writing stories which he will put in Natalia's trunk when she gets married, and which will amuse them on their honeymoon.'

'28 February 1881: Today he said to me: "I think I've found my subject. It's called 'Difetto Moderno' ('A Modern Fault')." That was all he said.'

This continuous process of conceiving, accepting and rejecting subjects meant that Ettore was all the time, almost unconsciously, selecting. And in a page of self-criticism, which bears the date 24 February 1881, he draws up a balance-sheet of failed enterprises and expresses the anxieties that gnaw at him, and his endless inner trial.

HISTORY OF MY WORKS

1. *Ariosto the Governor*. More thought about than written. I believed I had worked out all the details so well that this first effort was going to be a masterpiece. How I let my wishes deceive me! I didn't even finish the first scene, because that was where I realized the abstruseness of the idea and the wretchedness of the style.

1. The plateau which lies above Trieste.

2. *Stonature d'un Cuore* (*Discords of the Heart*). One scene of this has survived, and it makes me blush. Conventional phraseology, clumsy development, prose that would like to be poetry and isn't even prose. The *dénouement* (at least the idea of the *dénouement*) seems to be logical but impossible. I ought to have dedicated it to the Chinese – it was like their favourite *Hoci-lai-ke*.[1] The title is tragic; the play looked like being comic.

3. *La Rigenerazione* (*Regeneration*). I wrote two acts of this, I regret to say. It was the sort of thing that might have done as a one-act play, and I wanted to stretch it out into four.

Elio continued to make notes: '10 March 1881: Ettore is writing a story, "Tre Caratteri" ("Three Characters"), and I think he thinks of publishing it in the *Indipendente* when it's finished.'

But Ettore's ambitions were growing and his plans broadening. '14 March 1881. Ettore is beside me writing "Three Characters".' '5 April 1881. It will be called "La Gente Superiore" ("Superior People"), Ettore now tells me, giving me the usual, ever solemn news that he has burnt a play and is now writing another.'

Elio, the only person who believed in his brother's talent, discusses his doubts and spurs him on, gets impatient, complains about the obstacles strewn in his way and fears the fluency which carries Ettore from subject to subject, and his feeble will-power in sticking to his task. He is always afraid on Ettore's behalf.

'12 May 1881. Ettore does . . . nothing: he reads, he keeps studying, and he's more and more determined to study and to write. He's full of dreams of plays and other works, sometimes dramatic, sometimes novelistic, which never get down on paper. He's now changed his outlook on art: he's a realist. Zola has confirmed him in the idea that the object of

1. *The Circle of Chalk* (*Hui Lan Chi*) by Li Hsing tao.

drama and its interest must lie in the characters and not the
action. Everything must be true.'

'2 June 1881. Today I had a little quarrel with Ettore. For about four years I have been following his progress in literature with real interest. I am sorry to see that although he keeps studying, he writes nothing serious and in my opinion he won't achieve his aims unless he achieves some success which makes Papa allow him to study and encourages Ettore himself. The way he's going he'll give up his studies in the end, because he'll lose all hope of overcoming the difficulties he'll meet on the way to becoming a writer. I thought this, but told myself that, after all, if Ettore was still studying nothing was lost. That is, I thought it until the other day, when he told me he had to neglect his work at the office in order to study. I then told him what I thought, and he said nothing to me at the time; but when I asked him what he had done during the night he replied that it was none of my business and that, seeing how encouraging I'd been, he wouldn't read me anything else. So that was how it ended. But yesterday evening he read me one of his poems.' (No trace of any poetry has remained among his papers.)

'19 November 1881. Ettore has written an article which has been published in the *Indipendente* and republished in the *Gazzetta drammatica* in Milan.'

This is the last time Elio mentions Ettore's work. He was ill with nephritis, which gradually removed him from us. The diary becomes nothing but a lament. A journey to Cairo in 1885, made in the hope of a cure, took him even further away. He died in September 1886, just twenty-three years old, after a terrible illness which had lasted three years. For Ettore his death was a tragedy. He lost not only his favourite brother but the person in whom he confided his literary dreams, the one in whom he saw himself reflected, never to be replaced by anyone else.

Ettore preserved Elio's diary jealously, the diary in which the kindly unfortunate boy had put down his dreams and declared his firm faith in Ettore's destiny as a writer. Elio's early death left Ettore with a vein of melancholy which he never lost: indeed, as the family suffered other disasters it became worse. His sisters suffered too. Paola was unhappily married. Noemi died of puerperal fever, leaving a little girl, who was to die within a few years, in the care of her grandparents; then Natalia gave birth to two children who were deaf mutes. In 1897, Ortensia died within three days of being struck by a sudden illness, leaving a son a year old, Umbertino. Ettore's spirit became more and more downcast. He accepted the fact that suffering was an inevitable part of life, but even in his happiest years, those after his marriage, this melancholy never disappeared. Even art could not raise his spirits.

What he wrote on 19 December 1889 shows a profound bitterness:

Today I am 28. My dissatisfaction with myself and with other people couldn't be more complete. I note this impression down, in case some time in the future I am able to look back and either call myself a fool for writing in this way (things being even worse by then) or cheer myself up, finding I am not as bad as I was. The money question gets worse and worse; I'm not happy about my health, about my work, or about the people round me. And as I'm not contented with my work, it's perfectly reasonable that no one else should be either. But with all the enormous ambition I once had, not to have found anyone, *anyone at all*, to take an interest in what I'm thinking or doing; to spend my time having to take an interest in other people's doings as the only way of getting a little attention for my own. Two years ago exactly I began that novel which was to have been God knows what; and in fact it's a disgusting mess and will choke me in the end. My real strength always lay in hoping, and the worst of it is, I'm even losing my talent for that.

Here he refers to all the things that saddened his youth, the
economic worries of his large family, which in the past had
been used to a very different way of life. They all struggled to
keep up a decent standard, oppressed by the incurable
melancholy of their father who could not adapt himself to
poverty. Moreover, a gnawing doubt in his own intellectual
and physical strength had already taken hold of Ettore. He
worried about illness, and did so increasingly over the years.
He feared for his lungs perhaps too much, yet could never
give up smoking. After Elio's death his inner loneliness
became ever greater, and he badly needed recognition and
understanding. Deep down, hidden from everyone, he was
pierced by two things – the longing for fame, and a lack of
confidence in his own work, to which he could give only part
of his time.

The book which Elio had waited for, and had not seen,
appeared in 1892, a thousand copies published by the small
firm of Vram in Trieste at the author's expense. In 1890 a
long story called 'L'Assassinio di Via Belpoggio' ('Murder in
Via Belpoggio') had appeared in the *Indipendente*, but he
thought little of it. His first book was a novel, and called *A
Life*. It seems to have been finished by 1889. Entitled *Un
Inetto* ('The Inept One') it was offered to Treves, the Milan
publishers, who refused to publish a novel with such a name,
and Ettore had to wait until he could bring it out at his own
expense. He did not keep the pseudonym of Samigli but,
reflecting his German and Latin origins, appeared before the
public as Italo Svevo. It was not so much the blood he had
inherited which made him choose that pseudonym as his
memory of the cultural influences he had received in
adolescence in Germany, where the influence of Schopenhauer had been the strongest. Throughout his life Schopenhauer was and remained his favourite philosopher: he owned
his complete works and often quoted whole passages from
memory.

There was something of Ettore's character in the passive,

timid hero of *A Life*. Alfonso Nitti, the bank clerk, brought no enthusiasm to his grey, everyday work – only passive resignation, knowing that only artistic creation could give him the satisfaction he was seeking. The careful descriptions of life at the bank and the two evening hours spent reading in the public library are also autobiographical.

Ettore awaited the critics' response in a fever. By writing in the *Indipendente* he had achieved some fame as a literary critic in the city's small cultural circle, but he wanted to be known as a writer in a much wider world. A letter arrived from Paul Heyse, an anti-naturalist and leader of a circle of Munich writers, who was interested in Italian literature.

'Munich, 19. IV. 1897

'Only today, my dear sir, is it possible for me to thank you for your novel *A Life*, although I read it several weeks ago in the pleasant idleness of Salò on Lake Garda. I often get books sent to me from Italy, so many that it is not possible for me to write at length to every author, indeed sometimes not even with a word of thanks. If I make an exception for your book it means that the talent I have found in it has interested me a great deal, and I have seen only too well that deep, serious work goes unnoticed in Italy. First of all, this novel falls into the same mistake as almost all the Italian novels I have read in the last ten years. I find such a profusion of words in it that it could easily be reduced by half without injuring anything essential, eliminating superfluous details and endless repetitions; and further, you haven't yet realized the necessity of subordinating the secondary figures so as to bring the principal ones into relief. You are tireless in describing the most insignificant procedures of life at the bank. The secondary figures are developed with as much loving care as the leading ones, as if what you were aiming at was a scientific exercise *à la* Zola.

'And what is more to the point, the hero of your novel is so weak, so insignificant, that occupying oneself so persistently

with him and his *milieu*, analysing his minutest feelings, his
thoughts, his soul, seem not really worth the trouble. If,
despite that, I read your book to the end it is because,
notwithstanding these defects, which may be attributed to a
false artistic theory on the part of modern naturalism, I found
in it a serious research after truth and a consistent devotion to
psychological problems. If you were to choose a theme which
would allow you to apply these gifts to a happier and more
significant subject-matter, and would keep a severer control
over your narrative, you would certainly win a place among
the best novelists of the day.

   'With all good wishes
    'Paul Heyse.'

A review also appeared in the *Corriere della Sera* by
Domenico Oliva, and articles in the Trieste press. Then there
fell an inexplicable silence. The edition was sold out more
through gifts to friends than through purchases by the
general public. Ettore was dismayed at his lack of success. A
few critics had reproached him for the poverty of his
language and thus wounded him cruelly. He had longed to
give up his poorly-paid job and to go to Florence, there to
take up his studies again in language and literature. But the
book's failure put paid to his dreams. The chain had
tightened on him and his lack of self-confidence increased.

A month after our engagement he gave me the book, in
which he had written:

To Livia, a bad binding and a bad book. But, all the same, an
unusual gift for a bride. For this reason, and for it alone, I am
glad to have gone through so much in writing and publishing it.

In about 1890, Ettore's heartfelt loneliness was broken
when he met Umberto Veruda, a gifted young painter who
was revolutionizing nineteenth-century painting in Trieste,
but was still not understood there. Trieste was a business-

man's city, scarcely aware of art at all, certainly not with any depth. There was no understanding of the new painting and its use of light. In Ettore, who was older than himself, Veruda found a brotherly spirit. For many years their understanding was complete, and they lived in mutual harmony. When they were both in Trieste, after Veruda's frequent journeys to Munich, Vienna, Paris or Berlin, they would meet two or three times a day. In the evening Veruda would wait for Ettore in his office and while away the time sketching the passers-by. They would stroll along the Corso, and spend hours at night together in the Caffè dei Portici di Chiozza, where the Trieste intellectuals gathered. They confided their hopes in each other and encouraged each other. Knowing that he was understood, Veruda could talk to Ettore about the exciting problems of the new school of painting, and Ettore would spend hours in his friend's studio in Via degli Artisti, where Veruda painted with his faithful, enthusiastic pupil, Ugo Flumiani.

Ettore and Veruda had much in common. Both felt misunderstood by the conformist provincials around them. Both were swimming against the tide, and were oppressed by profound melancholy, which Veruda tried to escape by abandoning himself to wild gaiety at Saturday parties of the Artists' Club. Both had great courage and little education. Both felt surrounded by suspicion and disagreement. Their fine friendship lasted fourteen years, mingling their two spirits: Ettore tempered Veruda's strange outbursts with his own mild cheerfulness, and sweetened his sharp tongue; while Veruda, with his instinctive self-assurance, taught Ettore, bowed under the blows of fate, to smile at life in spite of everything. After Ettore's marriage the bond between them weakened. Veruda had been displeased to hear of his engagement, fearing that his friend would move away from him – which, in some ways, he did.

Veruda died in 1904, at the age of thirty-seven. For the past year, with an inexplicable presentiment and agony, he had felt death approaching. Ever since he had seen his mother die, angry with him, he had been oppressed by a feeling of misfortune. He fled to Paris, where he went about with his pockets full of letters and addresses to establish his identity if he were to die suddenly. He no longer painted. Worried about him, Ettore offered him hospitality in our peaceful house at Murano, which my mother had built beside the paint factory. 'You can work there,' he wrote, 'you'll find confidence in yourself again, in art, in life.' Veruda accepted the invitation, came close to Ettore again, and showed fondness for me too; and in the peaceful lagoon creative power returned to him. In order to work better he moved to Burano, and in a few weeks had almost completed two large paintings for the next international exhibition in Venice: 'Commenti' and 'Fondamenta a Burano'. But in this last refuge the illness he had been nursing so long burst out pitilessly. He returned quickly to Trieste, leaving the sketch of a 'Testa di Buranella', and died on the night of 19 August 1904. That day I saw Ettore for the first time lying on his bed, weeping like a child. Once again he had lost a friend, a spiritual brother, the one to whom he confessed his secret thoughts and who had been close to him in all the setbacks of life.

It was he who took care of Veruda's father, alone, blind and unsupported, until he died. In October 1904 he and Enrico Schott put on an exhibition of all Veruda's work in a pavilion built at the end of the Grand Canal, beside the church of Sant'Antonio Nuovo, thus giving the dead painter the universal approval he had never had while alive. Ettore was heir to the paintings, which he brought to our home, and in his will stipulated that the collection should not be broken up. During the Second World War I only just managed to rescue them, taking them to Arcade, in the province of Treviso, where I had taken refuge with my daughter Letizia and my grandson Sergio in August 1943. Ettore felt his friend was intensely alive in all these works. But with his spontaneous laughter and downright way of seeing things, Veruda also lives on in the pages of *Senilità* (*As a Man Grows Older*) where many of his characteristics are found in the sculptor Balli. And a scene in *As a Man Grows Older* in its turn inspired Veruda's masterpiece, 'Portrait of the Sculptor', which is in the Gallery of Modern Art in Venice.

Many years later, writing to a close friend, the painter Emerico Schiffrer, Ettore described the figure of Veruda:

14.6.28

Werter Freund Schiffrer,

When I try to recall Veruda's character, the first thing that strikes me is that it is radically different from that of Balli, at least when he arrived here from Munich, after Naples and Rome.

At nineteen he had already experienced the dangers of life, and he had relations with women when he could, but carefully, in a cautious way as with things that can burn. He already had the responsibility of keeping his own little family with its head above water, and it wasn't easy, with only a single source of income; that is to say oil-paint. So he was altogether different from the confident and inartistic Balli. Unlike Balli, too, Veruda had had artistic success from the start. Success with women, too, who love men who have made a name. But I never discussed love with Veruda, and for years we had no women with us. Then love came to me, and soon afterwards something like it also happened to him, though it ended with his departure for Vienna without regrets and without further drama. I know that the peak of drama came for him when he slapped his mistress's face in public in the Politeama[1] – something she boasted about for a long time. He did of course resemble Balli in some things, as Benco has said so well: great loyalty, but also a certain indifference to the things of this world if they are not beautiful.

If there was tragedy in Veruda's life, it came on him

1. The Politeama Rossetti was the Trieste opera house.

through the death of his mother at Villacco. For love of her,
too, he never thought of further complicating his life. For a
time he thought of marrying for money. It became a great
joke with him. Whenever there was a notable marriage in the
city, he would work out how much he had lost. A million,
two million, once even three. No one could lose millions as
casually as he did. It was always said about him that he was a
great fighter. But he preferred the company of unsuccessful
writers like me, of a doctor,[1] brilliant but eccentric, and of a
slightly strange clerk, to that of the rich, who might have
been patrons and paid no attention to my advice.

Ettore was no longer alone, though: he found his centre in
a family.

On 20 December, at home, we celebrated our engagement.
Until then he had not thought of marrying. After his
mother's death he had continued to live in the family home,
cared for by his sister Paolina, a cultured, intelligent and
good woman, whom an unhappy marriage had forced back to
her old home with her three children, Davide, Sarah and
Aurelio. Her care of Ettore, Adolfo and the youngest, her
sister Ortensia, was truly motherly. The others had left the
nest, each now having a home and family of his own. Ottavio
had been far away for years, a banker in Vienna, married to
Federica Freiberger, an outstanding pianist around whom
clustered the best musicians in the city. Enterprising, serious
and honourable, Ottavio had inherited all his father's best
qualities. Adolfo, although he continued to work in the
family firm, was mad about music and temperamentally
drawn to fanatical patriotism.

At thirty-four, Ettore seemed settled in the groove. But
then he fell in love, almost without realizing it, and it was the
greatest event of his life. Only his mother, a few years earlier,
had guessed at our destiny. One day, looking out of the
window as we went out side by side, she had said: 'Those two
go very well together.'

1. A Doctor Marcus, of Germano–Austrian origins.

The period of our engagement was one of intense disturbance for Ettore which he tried to allay by smoking, and of acute insomnia. His sensitivity was extreme. One day he actually said to me: 'Remember that a single ill-chosen word would be the end of everything.' Being engaged to a woman so much younger than himself, he was tormented by acute, I would almost say morbid, jealousy. Everywhere he saw shadows. To communicate more intimately with me, he wrote me a letter on 23 December 1895, which was the beginning of a diary which he kept until the eve of our wedding.[1]

23.12.1895

My Livia,

So, thanks to that good idea of yours, I can put down my own pure dream on paper! So pure it quite frightens me! So pure I sometimes wonder whether it can really be about love, for I've known love in quite a different disguise. If only you knew how different! I won't describe it, because if I did I couldn't send you this letter. But to think that I, who thought myself the end product of a century's ferment – a creature that cannot continue because all it knows how to want with any intensity is peace or hasty satisfaction, something stolen and quickly forgotten, a shameful act of theft, comforting in a cowardly way – that I can be at your side and, to convey the unheard-of purity of my own mind, should feel like saying, as I kiss you, a word which amazes even you: 'Sister!' It is amazing ! The word wasn't well chosen, I agree, but where can I find another? 'Lover,' I shall never say: it is truly the word I hate most, because it reminds me of faces I now hate. All this will pass, because life will once again smother us in all its vulgarity and perhaps (oh poor Livia!) I shall once again become the person who tortures himself, and anyone close to him, with his own doubts and his own past, all those painful experiences which are never forgotten because they have

---

1. Published as *Diario per la Fidanzata*, edited by B. Maier and A. Pittoni (Edizioni dello Zibaldone, Trieste, 1962).

become part of one's flesh and one's nerves. In the meantime,
though, this year, or rather these ten or eight months, will be
like these first forty-eight hours and will appear to me as a
pause in my life in which the physical laws were less severe
and the ever-wintry landscape was warmed by a sun I didn't
know existed. So, a bonus! If something else comes later (oh,
the duet in *Otello*!) we can always console ourselves, above
all, by remembering the day when St Thomas seized on St
Anthony to tell him his doubts and St Anthony told him
(which was odd for a Father of the Church) that it wasn't his
business to remove doubts. How sweet you were! I, as a
dilettante (not, unfortunately, an artist) so enjoyed making
you suffer and I finally said to you 'I'm glad to have spoken to
you', while my unconscious mind told me I was glad to have
made you blush and grow pale, and enjoyed, like a conquest,
every movement which revealed hesitation or suffering in a
person usually so calm and confident! You must understand
me! I knew how to be so calm and cold in those testing weeks
before it all happened because I knew you were suffering,
and to hear that you had wept gave me hours of simple
happiness. Purer, my love may have become, and may be less
wild, but gentler? – no! And who knows but that if later I
should suspect you were trying to withdraw from me, even
the least bit, I might not feel like drawing you back to me by
making you weep. There's no more intimate relationship
than the one between a sufferer and the inflicter of suffering.
Every tear in your eyes (green? I really don't know what
colour that is) is a gift to me. I've been working on this letter
for whole days, and heaven knows what I've written. I've
changed so much in these last hours that if I reread it I might
tear the whole thing up, but it's better there should be a relic
of what is past. Finally, like a good accountant, I want to
draw up the bill. The first kiss, I gave you as coldly as I would
have put my name to a contract; the second, I gave with
enormous curiosity to analyse you and myself, but in fact I
didn't analyse anything and understood nothing, as I was still
feeling a kind of timidity that froze me; at the third kiss, and
those which came after it, I could feel in my arms the sweet

girl I had been searching for, and all that was left of my youth. Now, I understand the whole business less and less: what's certain is that my powers as analyst are not what I thought they were. I don't know the colour of your eyes, your hair often surprises me, and I still don't really know your kisses. Mine too have a strange quality: not passionate warmth, to be sure, because I'm careful, very careful, that they shall not be more than you allow them to be. I don't want to be violent, I want to be gentle and kind. My greatest pleasure lies in feeling that I've changed – I don't dare to say grown young again. Dear Livia, it has been a grave shock from which I have not yet recovered. But I do not worry too much; first of all because, with the goodwill I bring it, I shall probably recover, and secondly, even if I don't, things will be no less beautiful. It is already clear to me that you will never find another husband for (there is no point in hiding it from you) I've compromised you fatally and no one would have you now. And I've got another idea, too, but I won't put it down on paper. I'll tell you about it face to face.

Nunc et semper,
    Your
    Ettore.

This was how he started the first page of his diary:

A man can have only two great pieces of luck in this world: that of loving a great deal or else of fighting victoriously in the struggle for life. One may be happy in one or other of these but it doesn't often happen that fate allows both these happinesses. So it seems to me that happy people are those who can give up love or else withdraw from the struggle. The very unhappy are those who are split in their wishes or in their actions between opposing sides. It is strange that when I think of my Livia I see both love and victory.

Sometimes, beside a date, a note appeared: '7 minutes past 4'. This was the hour at which his mother died. At that time he often decided to smoke his last cigarette which, alas, never was the last. Perhaps by smoking he tried to quieten the 'frogs', which was what he called the insistent doubts that tormented him.

25 January 1896. Thank goodness, your mother rang me up to say that you're better, that love is curing the 'frogs'. Whereas I've got them twice as badly as before: on your account and on mine. Yesterday Piero told me that it's only a step from a cold to bronchitis, and the whole evening, and then later, at the *Piccolo*,[1] and later still in bed, I felt my Livia close, close to bronchitis. Do you know what it is like? Breathlessness and a fever that wouldn't let you even think of me, who'd be beside you, yours more than ever because I would be going through the same distress, the same fever, and you would die without even remembering that you were leaving me so wretchedly alone – for then I really would be wholly, wholly alone. I'm already so used to thinking of you as the pivot on which all my desires and hopes turn. Today is a clear fine day and when there's no scirocco my frogs keep quiet. I remember that yesterday I felt your pulse. Tick, tock! There was nothing tired or uneven about it. It was as calm and healthy as if it had to go on to eternity. I shall always remember it and so, when my frogs decide to croak again, I shall imagine myself as the one dying and you as the good companion of my bedside. You're already destined to become a nurse, and so you shall be. I'll be full of demands and ill temper and I'll make you suffer so much that when I peg out I'll leave you ugly and old and no one will want you.

This idea of being cancelled out after his death by a second marriage never left him. Even during the years when we lived happily together it kept returning insistently. He always felt posthumous jealousy of a presumed rival, and even wrote a humorous sketch about it.[2]

1. Like *L'Indipendente*, *Il Piccolo* was a leading paper of the irredentist movement. Svevo worked there in the evenings, reading the foreign press.

2. A two-page sketch entitled 'Livia', published in *Corto viaggio sentimentale e altri racconti inediti*, edited by U. Apollonio (Mondadori, 1957), pp. 425–6.

3 February. I've got a heap of things to do but I want to put down some of my impressions of your dear letter, ma bien aimée!!! Never have I been so clearly aware of my inferiority in matters of love! Oh, in order to become equal to you, with your simplicity of expression, it wouldn't even be enough to be healthy and strong! You love simply, and in your healthy mind this new thing settles down with all the other good, chaste things which shelter under your fair hair, and so it all adds up to something good, chaste, sincere and absolute. How different I am! The thought of you is every so often chased away by the thought of myself. What would it matter if, in exchange for all the joys you give me, I had to suffer a little through jealousy or social inferiority? Nevertheless, when I think of you making me suffer, I immediately love you less. You've had the letter I wrote to you, and read those pages too. How insincere their expression is compared with yours, my dear Knospe;[1] how laboured the thought is, how ideas keep getting preference over feeling! I almost feel as if I love in the way I played when I was twelve, with a terrible fear of being called childish! As I write, I have tears in my eyes from the pain of not being more like you, but no sign of them will reach the paper. The terrible speech-maker who lurks inside me always gets the upper hand and blurs all I want to say. The whole thing's more serious than you can realize, dearest Livia. But don't be afraid. I shall love you always, so far as the *fin de siècle* will allow – so much and no more. Maybe, in spite of my being near you, you'll keep the frank, simple speech which is your destiny. That way you'll prove once again that you're incorruptible. Let's hope you never come to seem like me!

The last entry, that of 6 March, included this:

Livia Veneziani, born for Schmitz.

She is blonde, there's no doubt about that; but in spite of her pale face and green eyes she might perfectly well have

---

1. German for bud, rosebud.

been born dark, which would have made her no less Livia
and no less born for Schmitz. Where did all this hair come
from, which doesn't seem destined for that delicate little
head? Sometimes the whole little figure seems top-heavy, like
a pagoda. Where did that contralto voice come from? Good,
deep, threatening, it stays mild and good so often and one
can't imagine how. It is harmonious but not in harmony with
the colouring of face and hair. Oh, how blonde dear Livia is
in her feelings!

We met every day and spent enchanting hours in the
garden of the Villa di Sant'Andrea.[1] He often came on his
bicycle, bringing me iced coffee. He was very lively, keeping
me constantly entertained with a string of amusing stories,
and often played pig-in-the-middle with me and my girl
cousins. He was happy and his humour bubbled like spark-
ling wine. We read Goethe's *Roman Elegies* together at that
time.

Our wedding took place on 30 July 1896. Because my
mother wished it, it was celebrated with some ceremony and
in the presence of many relations. We left at once for our
honeymoon, which lasted a month. Our first stop was
Annenheim on Lake Ossiach, and then we went on to Vienna
to meet my brother-in-law Ottavio. We then returned to
Trieste, passing through Fiume. During the journey Ettore
read me the first three chapters of *As a Man Grows Older*.

Our small apartment had been prepared by my mother on
the second floor of the Villa Veneziani. Her demanding
affection did not allow a complete break with me. After their
return from France, my parents had set up a factory near
Servola, not far from the timber docks, for the manufacture
of underwater paint. Beside the factory, in the fields, stood
an old house belonging to my maternal grandmother Fanny.
My father made plans for its restoration, and gradually, as his

1. The Villa Veneziani was in the Passeggio di Sant'Andrea.

wealth increased, it was made more attractive and more comfortable. He designed the plaster mouldings in the music-room (all light, in Venetian eighteenth-century style), with its grand pianos, and the fruit-and-flower motifs in the windows, and the Murano-glass lanterns on the verandah. It was the only residential building in an industrial area, among the office blocks, warehouses and square-built factories constructed later. Being intelligent and open-minded, my parents wanted their home to stand close to the factory, which meant that my mother as well as my father could keep a careful check on the work, and a friendly relationship was forged between them and the workmen and technicians.

Wistaria climbed over the pergola and the balconies and decorated the front of the house. The hall was quite small, the dining-room spacious, with magnificent coloured windows and lamps made of deer-horn from Russia. After that came the large music room, the verandah and two drawing-rooms with soft sofas, cushions and carpets. Behind the house was the garden with the bowling-green and tennis-court made in the years that followed, for the new generation. On the first floor lived my parents with my sisters Fausta and Dora, and my brother Bruno, who was still a child. This was the kingdom of my mother, who was small, dry and nervous: thus did she appear to guests beside the tall, placid figure of my father, whose beard flowed over his chest.

Such, for thirty-two years, were the home, surroundings and workplace of Ettore Schmitz-Svevo. Now nothing is left of this building but a heap of ruins: on 20 February 1945 our beloved home was destroyed by high-explosive and incendiary bombs.

Our second-floor apartment was modest, consisting of three rooms, and in this small flat with its windows looking on to the sea, we spent five very happy years. Ettore's life continued quietly between the house and the bank. He kept to a strict timetable. He had to give up his evening work at the *Piccolo*, where for many years he had read the foreign newspapers, but he continued to teach commercial correspondence in French and German at the Revoltella Institute, the future university of Trieste. It was his ambition and his pride to provide for his family with his own earnings, without taking anything from my relations. To help our finances I too for a while had an administrative job in my father's factory.

But money was unimportant to Ettore. When we became engaged, he told me: 'Remember, I'm not a money-making machine!' Every month he gave me his entire salary, only keeping back a small sum for his own few expenses. But he also never stopped working to help his brother Adolfo, who was head of the Schmitz firm and had fallen into financial difficulties, having stood surety for a friend for whom he had taken on a substantial burden. All these responsibilities weighed on Ettore's shoulders and prevented him dedicating himself to his art. We lived in close touch with my family and our many relations; the bonds between us were very strong. Every Sunday the Veneziani family received friends as well as relations, sometimes as many as a hundred. All musical and intellectual Trieste came to the house.

With marriage Ettore's life changed entirely. In the atmosphere of serenity and order which I created around him, I think he became less pessimistic. He relied on me entirely, rather like a child; I tried to make him tell me what he wanted in every way. I had to take him to the tailor, make him choose a new suit, and look after his clothes, for which he cared nothing. He nearly always wore black, and could not even undo the buttons of his shirt cuffs: he was absent-minded and never put things in their proper place; he liked things as simple as possible and had no wish for valuable tie-pins, cufflinks or rings. He was surprised I liked jewels, and wore his own wedding-ring only for a short time, then took it off, saying, 'It strangles me.'

In 1898 his second novel, *As a Man Grows Older*, was published, at Ettore's own expense, by the same publisher,

Vram. He had not really thought of publishing it: some of the chapters had been written six years earlier, as a means of educating Angiolina, the protagonist of the story, who was not imaginary, but a real person, a blossoming working-class girl called Giuseppina Zergol, who ended up as a circus rider. She was the first to read the part of the novel in which she appeared. Other characters were also taken from life, and their names were rumoured in Trieste. After our marriage, Ettore published it, waiting anxiously for a definitive verdict; but again it was greeted with a chilling lack of understanding.

Once again a letter arrived from Paul Heyse:

'Munich, 26 November 1898

'Dear Professor Ettore Schmitz,

'Thank you, dear sir, for the courteous gift of your second novel, which I read with the same interest that I felt in *A Life*. I found it contained the same art of psychological analysis, the same sharpness of observation.

'I only regret that you have wasted your talent on such a repulsive subject, for the story of a young man with so insignificant a life, without any moral backing, must surely so appear to you. Then, struggling wretchedly between illusion and clear judgement, he attaches himself with passionate obstinacy to a whore whose loss he mourns for the rest of his life. The problem of a love which overcomes even the deepest contempt and gives rapture and disgust at one and the same time may certainly be given poetic treatment. Turgenev used the subject in a masterly way in a short novel, *Petrushka*. But when you deal in tedious detail with the tiniest movement of his spirit, our pity for the hopeless wretch cannot long overcome disgust at his moral frailty, all the more so since the fate of his unhappy sister, who seeks a fatal consolation for her unsatisfied need for love, reveals it, by contrast, even more darkly. Are the emotional problems of strong, healthy natures so rare that the poet must seek his subjects in pathological cases?

'I should be happier to see you soon in a purer ambience rather than in this suffocating atmosphere of decadence.

'Yours sincerely

'Paul Heyse.'

No Italian paper mentioned the novel at all, apart from the *Indipendente* in a supplement.

Shaken by the public silence and indifference, Ettore wrote: 'I don't understand this incomprehension. It means that people don't understand. There's no point in my writing and publishing'; and sometimes he would add: 'Write one must; what one needn't do is publish.'

Sadly, reluctantly, he moved away from literature, hiding his bitter regret and only occasionally allowing it to show. He no longer spoke of plays or novels but slaked his thirst for them at night by reading. His liking for the French was transferred to Nordic writers. Ibsen, Dostoyevsky and Tolstoy now dominated his spiritual world. He was a slow but careful reader, and read from ten thirty onwards; after a couple of hours he would fall into a deep, calm sleep enlivened by dreams he never remembered.

His repressed literary longings sometimes returned to him and he would then write at any hour, in any place, on scraps of paper. At intervals he would make notes on thoughts and impressions, as if to peer more deeply into himself, and analyse his inner life more acutely. Then he would abandon these notes without correcting or elaborating them, and perhaps without reading them over. Those I was able to keep form part of his posthumous publications.

If *As a Man Grows Older* had brought him success, I am sure he would have carried on writing, even though the demands of the family prevented him from giving up his job to dedicate himself completely to it. He would fully have accepted a double life, and smilingly hidden the effort it cost from all of us.

When I told him I was to be a mother, he felt it so strongly that he had to write me a letter in which he analysed his new, unsuspected feelings:

Trieste, 8.1.97. 9 in the morning
The birth of Francesco Schmitz:

Yesterday, when she told me, she was still doubtful but already moved and agitated. Today we are almost sure: Francesco Schmitz is born. For five months we haven't known whether to wish for it or fear it. We were both puzzled: her thoughts flew to our greatest worry: 'Meanwhile,' she said, 'we won't be able to pay our debts any more.' Yes, of course! Then they won't be paid! But this isn't our greatest worry. I have an intense bitter-sweet taste in my mouth. Bitter because I thought of the many dreams I had which will be dreamt all over again by someone else, someone like me. Perhaps he too, having a mind like mine, will start by dreaming of the destiny of Napoleon and, perhaps by the same analogy, he will have the destiny of Trevetti.[1] Oh, how absurd! I'll be born again with the same dreams of him and for him, to the very end. Bitter too, because I wonder whether my own bitter struggle has not marked him physically with depressing, degrading marks which I'll pass on to him. And, by the same reasoning, sweet. Dreaming and hoping begin again. Carry on! This is life! Probably in the extending of my egoism, which is what fatherly love will be for me, I shan't recognize myself and my own hope: that I've been like that and this will happen to me. You're made in my image, yet something quite different will happen to you! You won't even think like me! It's illogical, silly, but as soon as I love him, this is how I shall think. So I have lost the comfort of my own logic, the only advantage of my way of life.

But yesterday I was jealous, and I shan't be so again. Yesterday I smoked and drank and I shall never smoke or drink again.

He was expecting a son. He had already chosen the name Francesco for him, his own father's name. On our first

1. The proverbial nondescript clerk.

wedding anniversary he wanted us to have a photograph
taken, and after he had seen it he wrote a piece for me entitled
'Family Chronicle. Started on 12 August 1897 at 12 noon.'

Although it does not appear in this photograph, there is a
baby in it as well. The balustrade is there on his account; it
was a great idea of the photographer's. Of course, even if it
had been removed the baby would have been quiet just the
same, and the photographer would have had no difficulty in
photographing it. Then the person carrying it in her arms
would appear as she really is, no longer with the elegant
youthful shape her features would make one suppose. The
baby's been photographed, but still without a name! It's
called Letizia or Francesco, and we still don't know which we
prefer because we've made up our minds to like best
whatever we get. I'd have liked to see it by means of the
recently-invented Röntgen rays, but its mother refused a
photograph of that kind and I had to be content with this very
imperfect one. So I can say little, in fact no more than the
photograph says about it. It seems to have an impatient
temperament and struggles in its little prison, making sudden movements which already indicate a difference of
opinion with its mother, who tries to quieten it. She already
claims to know its character a bit, for she is preparing its cot,
its little clothes, its swaddling bands, as if she wasn't expos-
ing herself to the risk of getting it all wrong. Some time ago,
about some object I don't remember, she said: 'Yes, that'll
do, it's the kind of thing babies like.' I looked at it to see if
there was anything in it which revealed its nature, especially
suited to babies, and found nothing. I resigned myself to
buying the object in question, a chair in which the baby
would certainly not be able to sit at my age, thinking:
'Women who make babies must surely understand them.'

The obviously blonde woman who has the honour of being
photographed beside me was called Livia Fausta Veneziani
and has been my wife for exactly a year. I must say I'm

amazed that this has happened. She takes everything seriously: the cook, Maria, her husband, and life. The cook Maria is wrong from every point of view; but we're fonder of her than she is of us. She's our first cook, the provider of meals which always get cold because instead of eating we go round looking at our new home and all our new things. Whereas as far as she's concerned, we're her tenth employers and she cares no more for us than she did for the nine earlier ones. She likes company, the way a cat does, but knows that after us she'll find it again in service. Up to a point she's respectful, eats all the bread she can find in the house and, if she could find it, would drink all the wine; she'd prefer to live on bread, in fact, because she doesn't like meat. I don't know what else to say and she isn't in the photograph behind the balustrade. Even after a year my wife takes everything seriously. Her husband – good God! The father of her children! And all the other degrees of parentage too – all of them taken seriously! A mother is someone to whom we owe our lives, ditto a father, who's also the master of the mother and of all that surrounds us. She doesn't realize it, but I think that in this regard she has not got as far as the French Revolution yet, and a *lettre de cachet* from patriarchal authority, countersigned by the King, would not cause her much indignation. Think of it, the King! What an honour to be locked up by order of the King! First she greets the leader of the city council, then the leader of the diocese, and if they don't respond she doesn't mind, because they're the authorities who have to be greeted, and those who represent her have only a single duty towards us and that is to represent her. So, the world is a fine ideological construction, in which each of us has his place and must respect other people's places. As a sociologist, my wife is no evolutionist, because naturally people change but their roles remain the same. And there's really no social contract. The roles were born and the people who occupy them are born for them.

After all this, it can be seen how seriously my wife takes life, among other things. She occupies her roles, one after the other, with great seriousness. Even as a baby, I think, she had a certain dignity. Obviously the baby's occupation was to be sick, scream at night, and fall ill. Duties came later and, as far as I know, from the time she was very young my wife learnt how to distinguish her indoor clothes from her outdoor clothes, and didn't appear even at the garden door in indoor clothes, or fail to change out of her outdoor clothes the moment she got inside.

I really think this serious life of hers was divided neatly into periods, each one of which brought its joys and sorrows, because whenever she sees someone younger than herself she immediately remembers what she was like at that age. This gives her a great, very pleasurable sense of justice. She too, at that age, had the pleasure of contradicting the wishes of those in command, even if they were perfectly fair, the pleasure of breaking things to see what they were like inside, of jumping, dancing, and shouting, whereas I never remember having been irrational or at least, if I was, considering myself every day a new animal, I don't admit that I remember or justify what I did in the past. That day's animal had to be punished and I was all for punishing my unreasonable contemporaries myself.

'When I was like that', she often says, but never complainingly. There's another thing I don't understand, this lack of regret for the past. It makes me believe she is so fair towards the present as to set it impartially side by side with the past and look on them as the same. It might look like indifference but in fact it's an absolute and inexplicable *joie de vivre*. I stand amazed, sometimes, when I see how much she enjoys existing things, or, even more, the things she owns. What a capacity for happiness and unhappiness! To me the everlasting questions, not only of being and non-being, but of mine and thine, leave me so mortally indifferent that anything that happens to me may pain me, annoy me, make me weep, but doesn't surprise me. Basically, what is there to be surprised about? Rocks fall, well, so do stars; the earth may split open, but we knew there was fire inside it. The whole of humanity may change and be made up of saints or murderers, but we knew it might happen because a part of it has always been so.

She, on the other hand, hears every day of new things, things which surprise her and make her thoughtful. No doubts, though! There's no room for them. Prayers, at the appropriate time, are listened to up there; very often they aren't granted, but in that case people know at least they have done what they should and can feel calm.

That, being constructed as we two are, we should be together is even more amazing. Just consider it: made for rebellion, indifference and corruption as I am, always admiring what might be and never respectful of what is, I married, convinced that I was making a new experiment in sociology, the union of two equal beings linked by an inclination which might be momentary, a union in which jealousy must be banished by knowledge, that is to say resignation to things and feelings as they are; a union which didn't really demand that either of us should change, because to be together doesn't in the least mean you must resemble each other. I got married, certain that if one of us was going to change, it wasn't going to be me! In fact, I wanted to change my wife a little, in the sense of giving her freedom and teaching her to know herself. I got some books by Schopenhauer, Marx, Bebel (*Woman*),[1] intending not to press them on her, but gradually to insinuate them. But, in fact, literature, at least of the kind I particularly wanted, disappeared from our relationship. Only once did we discuss my ideas, and that was about Heine. To hell with that romantic whom once, in the heat of argument, I proclaimed my god! Then we left my ideas alone, and very adeptly and very gently avoided the subject. Good bourgeoise that she is, what matters for her is to live in peace with everyone and keep one's own ideas in one's own little head, protected by all that hair. She doesn't try to persuade. Whereas the rest of us are all apostles of some idea, or of the idea of *Nothingness*.

This I have to concede to her, and as I say it I don't know whether I feel admiration or anger. She has never persuaded anyone, but my home resembles her more than it does me.

1. August Bebel's *Die Frau und der Sozialismus* (*Woman and Socialism*), 1879.

It's very tidy, with beautiful objects in it which she likes a
great deal, and so of course I do too. Sometimes sacrifices are
made to procure some object which is felt to be needed, even
if only to replace one which serves its purpose perfectly well
but isn't very attractive. I agree, but I do worse: I argue and
even refuse. Some days ago she had a brilliant idea: she talked
of getting four gas stoves. I must explain that gas here costs as
much as if it were extracted from gold rather than coal.
Remembering good housewifely practice, I refused. There's
great pleasure in refusing something and in doing it like that,
as the absolute master, and I was amazed to realize that my
refusal, which was made as an interesting experiment, had
been taken seriously. So, I had my doubts, and now as a good
householder I'm considering whether it's a good idea to
install gas stoves. So you see I am a genuine *paterfamilias*.

In short, my wife, my parents-in-law, my cousins, male
and female, all say I'm a good husband, and the worst of it is
that when they tell me this I don't get angry.

Our daughter was born at dawn on 20 September 1897,
with her father's black eyes and hair. She was called Letizia
in memory of Ettore's mother, who had been called Allegra,
Fausta in honour of my sister who was her godmother, and
Pia in memory of 20 September, a special day for us
irredentists.[1]

After the birth, my health suddenly deteriorated. Many
cases of death from puerperal fever had taken place in Trieste
at the time, and the family was very worried. I had to stay in
bed for forty days. In the meantime, Ettore's youngest sister,
our beloved Ortensia, died from a sudden attack of
peritonitis. This sad news was kept from me, out of respect
for my illness, and even Ettore hid his sorrow. Before coming
into my room he would change his black tie for a coloured
one. One day he forgot to do so, and when I asked him about
his mourning tie he answered quickly that, having got ink on

1. 20 September 1870 was the day the Italian army entered Rome after
storming the Porta Pia.

his red one, he'd bought another. Thus even the joy of fatherhood was clouded by anxiety over my illness and mourning for his sister. As he wrote: 'Life cannot be understood unless accompanied by great joy and great sorrow.'

The baby grew splendidly and Ettore was full of fatherly tenderness. This appears vividly in a group of letters to me in 1899, when I was convalescing at Salsomaggiore. It was the first time I had been parted from him. I left the baby in the care of my sister Nella, who had returned from Bulgaria with her three children, Vela, Olga and Nico, and had come to live near us. Her husband, having given up his profession of engineer and his own country, had come into the firm to help my father as technical director.

In the morning I have coffee and Titina (nickname for Letizia) brought to my bed. The former I drink, the latter I make cry. In the evening I go and see Titina, and better than you because I don't wake her.

Titina is very good. She already calls Nella Mamma and you Zazalla. When she is asked where Mamma is she says: 'I don't know, she's gone out to get sweets for Titina.' And that's enough for her, selfish little thing. All I hope is that they don't spoil her while you're away. When she sees me she pretends to be happy but I don't believe it.

Humorously, he kept me in touch with the child's daily routine, which he observed at every level.

Titina's doing well. I never want to forget this phrase which – let's hope – will always be a cliché. Yesterday she dirtied herself with a certain yellow liquid manufactured by herself. Between yesterday and today I was with her for a whole hour and in this single hour she gave me evidence of her good upbringing and strong nerves. Nella scolded her and she said to her face quite calmly 'Bad mamma'. She also attacks Vela, Olga and Nico. She beats them and scratches them and makes them run away which, when you see it, is ironical. The small body which has only lately been able to stand upright on its own is already trying to knock others down. I asked Nella to give her an occasional slap, but she won't hear of it. Marco looks on and makes no move, but I realize that, like me, his hands are itching. But I make no move either. I look at this sprig of mine and don't know whether I should control it or let it grow like this, as a *flagellum dei*, more dangerous to others than to itself. And so Titina is developing, mistress of herself and of others, in a way absolutely opposite to the one I'd foreseen. She gives kisses when she needs something, and refuses them when she doesn't. She asks for things four times a minute, astonished that no one has flown to help and care for her. Ah, well! You offer her something, and she says 'yes' at once, her voice sweetly modulated in a way which is evidently an imperial command. And what about thanks? Well, she gives them, more or less, when you ask for them, but in a way that means: Go to the devil. When she's in bed, the house calms down. The birds then dare to go back to the horse-chestnut tree, and Tyras[1] moves more freely. Pronto[2] and the children who are still up at once play less nervously. Nella's colour returns. In the kitchen the maids speak more loudly and tell the others about the hard times they've had during the day. Bezzina, whose hair Titina tugs a little out of each day, says fearfully: 'Is she in bed?' 'Why?' I say, and he says 'The beauty!' I can't tell you the meaning of that 'beauty'! It's what, or more or less what, the ancients called Attila's wife, who, if she ever existed, ate a dish of children's noses for lunch sprinkled with parmesan. This morning I asked her for a kiss. She wouldn't give me one. Well, I'll be revenged, I thought. This letter is my revenge.

The second year I was having treatment I took the child with me. For the first time we left Ettore on his own: he wrote to me every day. He was very interested in the child's state of mind:

1. Gioachino Veneziani's Great Dane.
2. The Venezianis' black dog.

I'm much amused that Titina isn't satisfied with the slaps you give her and misses the ones I give her more and more each day. My little pet. How well she's understood, better than all of you, that the punishments I give her are sweeter than the caresses you give her, and she doesn't want to be without me; anyway, I've always said you're a swallow who hatched a cuckoo's egg and there's little in common between you and Titina. She's my daughter and you're a wife, but not her mother. Tell her that, and I bet she won't protest any more.

These letters brought us closer together.

Trieste, 17 June 1900

My dear, my kind, my sweet fair one,

I have just got up after a long, refreshing sleep. I dreamt that you were dead and had been laid on my bed in your coffin. You have no idea how happy I felt this morning seeing the sunlight and knowing that you were still alive after all, even if at Salsomaggiore. The dream must have been over in a moment, a fraction of a second. The coffin was dark and you were all shining inside it. The only occupants of the room were you, dead and motionless, with your eyes shut and your mouth obstinately set; your mother, who was running to and fro (even in a dream she couldn't keep still), bringing flowers to strew your corpse; and myself, studying your face, which bore a look of reproof, as if I hadn't brought enough joy into the life that had been entrusted to me. Your mother was bustling about as she does in the office. She kept arranging your great flood of golden hair round your stiff body. I thought: 'Why does she bother?' But in fact she was enjoying you quite as much as if you were still alive. I woke up overjoyed at being able to hope I could be the one to die first. I am still full of the sweet feeling it gave me and want to share it with you. I'm all alone in the house and shall give up the whole afternoon to my letter. I wouldn't go out, though it was Sunday, so that I could write it. I think I must have dreamed about your death several times before (you know how the idea of death is always in my mind), but never as vividly as

this. I am glad of the dream now, as I am of anything which
reminds me of the joy of possessing you. Possessing you fully
and legally. . . . You don't know what sacrifices I would make
to save you unhappiness. How could you, seeing that when
the jealous husband takes over I breathe fire and slaughter?
So your husband is your enemy, the husband who fails to give
you what is due to you and contrives to do you out of the
mildest enjoyment you might get from your own beauty. All
in all, I am a poor neurotic delinquent, and it makes me
unhappier sometimes than you can imagine. When you are
home again I want to see if I can't have more control of
myself. I have no hopes, and neither have you, that I can do
so on the matter of jealousy . . . only that's the very point
where I most want to. But it's no good. It's exactly those little
pleasures I have been talking about that I'm always going to
rob you of. But instead, I make you this formal promise. I
deny you those little pleasures of vanity which the mother of
Titina can cheerfully renounce, but I promise you formally
that if ever life offers you a great opportunity of happiness,
one of those a young woman might give up peace, virtue,
conscience and life itself for, I shall know how, granted that I
have your full confession (you know I tolerate everything
except lies), to put you in the way of having it. Having made
this declaration, which ought to make you feel freer, my
conscience is easier. What it amounts to is, I deny you the
right to trifle with your life and mine, but I don't forbid you
to turn your back on them altogether if something should
make it worth while. Indeed, I will hear your confession like
a father and we will discuss the situation to see how it can be
made to cause you the least possible suffering. Not a single
stupid word of rebuke. You wouldn't want me to kiss you any
longer, and I wouldn't try to.

Only like this, it seems to me, can our marriage be a free
Socialist union. You are to stay with me just as long as you
feel you should. Pay no attention to my silly petty jealousies;
they will always be over silly petty things. I promise you by
all that's dear to me you won't have to put up with a single
harsh word if you make me a confession about something

involving not your vanity but your happiness. I know this is sincere and comes from my deepest convictions.

'Salso, 19 June 1900, 2 p.m.

'My beloved,

'Your letter of Sunday morning breathes the deepest and sweetest love and makes me very proud and very happy; but it also expresses a harsh philosophy.

'No doubt you have all the qualities to make you a good brother, but you are also a very good husband. Believe me, my dearest, I have not suffered half as much from your jealousy as I have been given pleasure, exquisite pleasure, by your kindness and goodness to me. I am grateful to you from the depths of my heart and I bless you a thousand times over, thanking God for you.

'I utterly refuse the freedom you so generously offer me, I am bound to you by very strong and very sweet links which nothing will ever break now; I gave myself to you out of love, and I will never withdraw the gift. I thank you for all that you have given me and that you think of as so little – that ardent love which your very jealousy proves to me, that brotherly tenderness, that intense and sweet friendship which links us and will never perish and on which I mean to lean for the rest of my life. Don't think which of us will die first; let us hope we can die together, so as not to feel the agony of parting.

'My beauty (if it exists), and my youth, are for you alone; enjoy them to the full, in perfect confidence. It is not merely Letizia's mother, it is your wife, my dearest, who cheerfully renounces her little pleasures of vanity. If I am beautiful, I want to be so for you, for you alone. I want to spare *you* every kind of worry and pain too. In a word, I love you, and I refuse the freedom that you give me.

'Believe me, all the sweet emotion you felt in writing to me found an echo in my own heart and made me feel closer to you than ever.

'*Au revoir*, my beloved husband, my dear brother, my

sweetest friend, I kiss you – full of the tenderest feeling – with
my whole heart, and I wish I could give you a thousand times
as much happiness as I am able to.

    'Yours for ever,

      'the faithful Livia'[1]

---

1. Translated from the original French (the language of Livia's school
days in Marseilles), in which she generally wrote to Svevo.

IN 1899 VERUDA wrote to Ettore from Vienna:

'Dear Ettore,

'I have heard with great pleasure that you are changing your present job for another. But I assure you that despite my intelligence, which is not just rare but unique, I don't understand. I realize that from the financial point of view you would do well to leave the bank and give yourself entirely to literature, and I think this is what you mean to do; of course I support this idea of yours enthusiastically and I imagine Livia will be the third to find it an excellent plan.

'I, on the other hand, am hanging on to the idea that if I hadn't been born, many people who because of me call themselves lucky wouldn't be able to boast that they'd had their portraits done by me. I hope these lines will show you how I've become quite . . .

'Success until now has been silent here, very silent indeed since nobody mentions it, but financially things have gone as they never did before; so, dear Ettore, now that I've given you news of life in Vienna I'll say goodbye. What chapter have you got to? When are you publishing? Do you like the baby? To all you poor wretches who live in the ghastly place which by mere coincidence was and is my country, my most affectionate greetings, ciao, Veruda.'

The year 1899 involved a very important development in Ettore's life. At my parents' suggestion he gave up his job at the bank and entered the Veneziani firm. The salary of 300 florins a month at last gave him economic independence, which he was delighted to have in order to be freed from what he called slave labour. With relief he gave up his occupations and gave himself entirely to his new work, dividing his day between the works and the office. He got up at half past six, went to the factory at seven, and at midday came home for lunch. After lunch he rested at home for a couple of hours; all he wanted was a good armchair and a good cigar. Evenings

were often spent at the theatre, which he loved passionately.
We often went to the opera and the prose evenings at the
Teatro Verdi. His new job gave him satisfaction because it
brought him in touch with workers in the factories at Trieste
and Murano, with whom he loved to spend hours, and
removed him from the passivity and boredom of his work at
the bank. Literature was put aside, but not denied. On one of
the small sheets he wrote on to keep his thoughts continually
flowing and taking form, he analysed his literary work. It still
preoccupied him that year, and he mentioned the need to
deepen it all the time. Anyone who wants to be a writer must
train himself day by day, with constant exercise: that was his
conviction.

I believe, I sincerely believe, that there is no better way to
become a serious writer than to scribble every day. You have
to try and bring to the surface every day, from the depths of
your being, a sound, an accent, the fossil or vegetable
remains of something that may or may not be exactly
thought, that may or may not be exactly feeling, but a whim,
a regret, a sorrow, something genuine, pinned down in its
completeness. Otherwise, on the day you think yourself
authorized to pick up a pen, you will fall into clichés and the
'object' will escape you. In other words, apart from the pen
there's no salvation. Anyone who thinks he can write a novel
by putting down half a page a day and no more is completely
deceiving himself. On the other hand, this little, written
under the influence of a particular moment, of the colour of
the sky, of the sound of a voice of one of one's fellow-humans,
will never become anything beyond what it is: the sincerest
account of too-immediate and too-intense impression. We
must not think of stitching such pages together to make
something greater. Napoleon used to make a note of
whatever he wanted not to forget on a scrap of paper which he
later tore up. Tear up your papers too, you literary ants! Let
your mind linger over the words with which you once fixed a
concept, and work upon them, changing them as you wish, in

part or entirely, but don't let this first immature sketch of the thought harden into fixity and restrict all its future development.

He never talked to me about his torment or his obsessions, as if he wanted, through an agreement we had made, to keep me away from his tortured secret world, which I then never even suspected. To me he showed only his cheerful face. He wanted me always to remain calm, simple and without inner complications, as if to draw strength from this way of being of mine.

But the business life into which he had plunged limited the time he could give to artistic creation and thought more and more. Increasingly the businessman was taking over from the writer. And the day came when he gave a decisive farewell to literature. But this farewell – the result, he said, of iron decision – cost him suffering which he tried to keep secret from everyone.

Three years later, it seemed as if he had definitely given up his vocation. He thought he had moved away entirely from literature; yet he still wrote, and justified this writing as a way of deepening his own life:

December 1902: I am writing this diary of my life over the past years without any intention of publishing it. The ridiculous, damnable thing called literature has now been quite definitely cut out of my life. Through these pages I only want to understand myself better. My own habit – the habit of everyone without power – of being able to think only with pen in hand (as if thought weren't equally needed at the moment of action), forces me to make this sacrifice. So once again, my pen, poor rigid instrument, will help me plumb the obscure depths of my being. Then I will throw it away forever, and get used always to thinking in terms of action: on the run, fleeing from an enemy or chasing one, my fist raised to strike or to fend off a blow.

To avoid yielding to the temptation of writing, he took to

playing his violin with enthusiasm, an instrument which had become his indispensable, irreplaceable companion. It distracted him and, as he once confessed in something he wrote, it saved him from literature.

Suddenly a new element arrived to shake up his life, widen his horizons, and secretly to nourish the artist who, though buried, was still alive in him: travel. The firm had a wide range of business interests in Austria, Italy, France and England, so for commercial reasons he had to travel about Europe and stay abroad for long periods. His first important journey was undertaken in June 1902. First he went to Toulon, then on to London. He took his violin with him, and, alone in the city, enjoyed practising and studying for hours.

. . . from the violin I drew satisfactions which were the only thing that for nearly twenty years could make me cling to it. In Trieste I was able to organize an amateur quartet: a cellist of the first order, a first violin who was an excellent sight-reader, a viola player who was a musician of taste. The players were all very fond of one another: indeed, when I made a mistake and the whole quartet hissed like a lot of snakes, no one looked at me. I would crouch down and, like a real snake, try and find my tail, so as to bite it and punish myself. Friendship is a wonderful thing.

The freedom and novelty of travelling stirred him deeply. In a letter from Toulon he mentioned his intention of writing a small one-act play in the time he had free from visits to the docks and to officials of foreign navies. Perhaps the play *Un Marito* (*A Husband*) was already gestating; after 'The End' it carries the date '14 June 1903'. But *A Husband* is not a one-act play: it is his most important work for the theatre, a three-act play which contains the complex material of a novel. It was published in the review *Il Convegno* in 1931.

After he had spent two weeks in London I had to join him because he felt lost on his own and needed warmth and calm.

The difficulties his slight knowledge of English caused at every step depressed him. We interrupted our stay in London to take a trip round Ireland, where the wild beauty of the landscape enchanted him. An unforgettable memory for me was our stay at Queenstown in August 1901. From the terrace of the hotel we could catch a glimpse of the distant blue Atlantic, an intense blueness like that of the Mediterranean, which surprised me. Ettore had to go to Carrigoloo to supervise the painting of Lord Muskerry's yacht. I went with him to the little works and rested in the guard's house, a small house covered in bright fuchsias. The guard's fair-haired little girl would come out holding a lamb in her arms, which she would dip into the sea water. Even Ettore was calm, delighted with all that beauty and peace.

A new factory was set up at Charlton, a suburb of London, so Ettore had to visit England two or three times a year. He noted the details of his surroundings with delicate humour and was ironical about English conventions, which wore down his free spirit. Many years later, setting down his memories of London at length, he remarked acutely:

For my business I had often to spend several weeks in a particular district of London. I always find these visits strangely attractive. First of all, I discovered England late in life. In youth, one assimilates things more easily. A young man who goes to England for a couple of months soon loses his amazement; he becomes anglicized and looks at things with an indifferent eye, as if they were his own work. Whereas I, late-comer that I am, walk about the streets of London and look about me in a continual state of surprise, muttering: 'Oh, that's fine! Oh, that's great! Oh, that's horrible!' and on each particular visit one of these exclamations will predominate. The first time I went there I stayed three months in a very fine hotel in Russell Square, close to the City. Those were three months of admiration. I was accompanied by a Frenchman who was enthusiastic about the English and I admired the policemen, who were so

respected and respectable, the many luxurious music-halls,
the luxury of the conquerors of India at Covent Garden and
the tidiness of the crowded streets.

He was a sharp observer. This is how, in 1924, in a letter to
a journalist friend,[1] be briefly analysed the repercussions and
effects, both present and future, of the arrival of the first
Labour government in English political life.

London, 28.1.1924

Dearest Giulio,

I have today received your kind letter of the 23rd, the
contents of which greatly surprised me. What's up? Is it
possible in our country to cancel with impunity contracts
made through a lawyer? What do the lawyers say, then? It is
absolutely pointless for me to send you advice from here. I
hope that you'll know how to defend your interests (or
rather, those of others) and I'll be curious to hear how
things go.

I shall be here until half-way through March, if not longer.
The weather isn't too bad even if it isn't very good. It's the
usual foggy mild weather of summer and winter.

I'm flattered that you ask what I think about the new
Labour government. The only thing I can tell you for certain
is that for the present nothing new has happened. The
government has been installed with the usual formalities: top
hats, and even wigs for the government lawyers. I have seen it
even in the sympathy which surrounded it as soon as it came
into office. It was greeted with a sort of romanticism and
descriptions of the hard struggle ministers had undergone
before achieving this success. For the moment, criticism is
silent, hope and agreement are general. The ministers are
workers rather than socialists. They cannot be anything else
because they survive with the active support of the Liberals.
To give you an idea of the lack of antagonism to this new

1. Giulio Cesari, a nationalist journalist and life-long friend of
Svevo's.

event in English history, I must tell you that everyone thinks England has in this way found the solution to the two problems which are rending it: one is foreign policy, peace in Europe; the other is a matter of internal politics, unemployment. So they are flattered as if they were something quite unlike what they are. The *Daily Telegraph* is surprised that Snowden's wife is not in the government beside him as she is a woman active in literary matters and has always taken part in her husband's life and work. The whole nation feels especially sympathetic towards the women who, with their husbands and fathers, have now soared so high. Miss MacDonald has become the mistress of No. 10 Downing Street and says: 'It's rather a complicated house, but very nice.' The first woman Secretary of State, Miss Bondfield, has the sympathy of all the other women in Parliament. Lady Astor is against the socialists only because they didn't include Miss Bondfield in the cabinet: 'She was worth more than all of you.'

The fear is that MacDonald will do too well and that he'll have an absolute socialist majority at the next election. But elections in England don't go by names, but by policies, and in order to bring in a capital levy, for instance, the country's consent would be needed. Thus, when Baldwin wanted to include protectionism in his programme, he had to appeal to the electors, who showed him the door.

Nothing new has happened and at present even the rebels in India know this. MacDonald has shown them that they may achieve a great deal by constitutional means but that no English government will be moved by force.

Of course France will be more uneasy than it was with Baldwin's government but – I feel – this will prove that this government is more English than the previous one.

The dangers that threaten MacDonald come not from the middle-classes but from the socialists and communists. For the moment there's a truce with them too, but there's already talk of the traitor MacDonald and even in the cabinet there are elements which consider things differently.

I hope you will be able to use my droolings, but without
quoting me, for heaven's sake.

Give my warm greetings to Miss Aurelia.

Warmest greeting from your affectionate Ettore.

On the second trip we had a small house all to ourselves in a very quiet street of villas and gardens. During the week Ettore was at the factory and studying English, but Saturdays and Sundays were entirely our own. We went to the theatre, to museums, and to the wonderful parks. These pleasant stays, lasting two or three months, were repeated two or three times a year until the outbreak of the First World War. Letizia seldom came with us, but stayed in Trieste with her grandmother. In the peace of our London house, perhaps Ettore achieved complete happiness.

An obsessive self-analyser, some years after his first journey, during his fourth visit to London, he remarked gloomily on the way in which the happiness and vigour of first impressions diminished with the passing of youth:

3.4.05

IV journey to London

Here I am again on my IVth journey to London: until now, I have written nothing about four similar journeys, whereas before, in my slow trips between the Corso and the Barriera Vecchia, I observed so much. Ho, youth! And yet I think that only one important thing has disappeared from my thoughts: self-admiration. Today I still have the same method: objects are reflected in my mind with the same vividness, but they pass away and I no longer care about preserving the images they aroused in me. Perhaps this happens because, as I have been compelled to play the salesman with other things, I'm disinclined to be one, or try to be one, in regard to ideas. In short, I embellished my whole journey, like my whole life, with curious observations which I conveyed to those nearest to me in the best words I could find; but why hand on my observations and words to my descendants just to give them the trouble of disposing of them? The fact is that all I remember of the journey, as far as it concerns me, is the impression I had crossing Italy, France and England. Passing through so much life, though I do not love it, moves me nonetheless, and I wished all their fields a double harvest, so that their people should be rich and good.

He who since he was young had longed to travel, and remembered with intense pleasure his fleeting visit to Constantinople,[1] now wrote:

At every change of place I feel a great, an enormous sadness. No greater when I leave a place to which are linked memories, pains and pleasures. It is the change itself which upsets me, like the liquid in a vase which, when shaken, becomes muddy.

Perhaps it was his own spirit, which was always going deeper rather than wider; he no longer wanted his concentration distracted by the external aspects of the world. And yet so many voyages, so many contacts with varied people, matured the European in him.

More and more he clung to his home, where the family life ran calmly, equably, without upsets. He wrote to me:

Charlton, 5.12.1903

. . . I think that until now it has been a great blessing to me that you were born and that all that happens in my life, which has become – through your doing – so agitated and excited, is softened by the thought of you and my little girl. The worst becomes bearable and when there's joy it's doubled, because of you, who share it. I wish no more than to be able to continue our life as it has been until now, except for the

---

1. Shortly before his marriage Svevo visited Constantinople with his friend Giuseppe Vivante, who subsequently married Svevo's sister Natalia. Vivante, whose brother Fortunato was the director of the Trieste branch of the Union Bank of Vienna, was instrumental in Svevo getting a job there.

many, frequent separations to which I cannot reconcile
myself. It is true that a honeymoon period follows these
separations and that I become more in love with my wife. But
I don't want this. I want to love you always and, although
you, my little goat, have complained of it, even in the longest
time with you there hasn't been a single day in which I have
avoided your company, or wished it any the less. 'And be this
a seal to undeceive all men,'[1] and women too, including you.

It is true that the rough work I do sometimes makes me
long to retreat into myself with some reading that doesn't
concern me at all, or some violin practice in which only my
fingers are at work. You must remember how many years I
gave to this sweet habit and how now it is so often forbidden
to me. My custom of dreaming is really what gives me an
almost continuous serenity . . .

. . . And in order to show you how every year I'm ready to
sacrifice the thing I like best for you, because it helps me to
dream, I promise you, this year again, to smoke no more . . .

After five years we left our small apartment and moved
down to the first floor of the house to share my parents' life.
The other children had left home. My sister Dora was
married first, to Dr Giuseppe Oberti di Valnera, and then
Fausta had married Francesco Trevisani, and had left with
her husband for Russia. My brother Bruno, the only one of
the family who was not involved with the factory, was still far
away in Vienna and Bologna, studying chemistry and music.
My mother, left on her own with my father, was more
attached to me than ever, and wanted to feel we were even
closer. Her relationship with Ettore was cordial and affectionate. She thought very highly of him and trusted him a
great deal.

Every Sunday we took part in a big family lunch, to which
my mother invited all her daughters who were in Trieste,
with their husbands and children. For some years the

1. Dante, *Inferno*, xix.21: '. . . questo sia suggel ch'ogn'uomo
sganni.'

children's leader was my brother Bruno who, born eighteen years after my parents were married, was still a boy. After lunch he would organize their games in the garden or on the verandah, depending on the season. On Sunday afternoons my mother received a large number of guests, as well as the relations. All intellectual Trieste attended those parties. In the music-room the quartet of Jancovich, Dudovich, Viezzoli and Baraldi would play. Games and dances were organized for the young people.

Ettore was always present at these parties and treated everyone in a friendly way. On the surface he was jovial and merry, and had a way of keeping everyone in a good mood: his ringing laugh would often be heard round the crowded room.

The reception rooms were crowded with paintings in those days. Among them were the finest painters in Trieste: Veruda, Flumiani, Fittke, Grimani, Orell. It was Ettore who had opened the doors of our home to painting. He often patronized the artists of Trieste, and as an expert he would talk of the influence of Veruda on Fittke, another first-rate but unfortunate painter from Trieste who committed suicide.

Trieste, 27 April 1922

Dear Signor Del Conte,[1]

When I got back from London my son-in-law gave me the magnificent study of Fittke by Schiffrer. I think it is the best that has been written in this country about an artist of ours. As I read the study, I saw our poor friend again in my mind and understood him better. Fittke deserved a friend like Schiffrer and I am comforted to learn that he had one. To put down my own personal memories is entirely superfluous and I have already destroyed the few notes I had made about him. In fact, about Fittke as an adolescent I can say nothing except

---

1. An associate of Svevo's who specialized in selling pictures by Triestine artists.

that he had a courteous face and took in my lessons on
commercial correspondence politely, though I was not persuaded that he actually would. I have only one objection to
make of this study. At a certain time in Fittke's life Veruda's
influence upon him must have been greater than Schiffrer
supposes it was. Later in Fittke's development perhaps the
first influence was forgotten and overlaid by others. I can
even pinpoint the time: immediately after his return from
Munich. The two painters worked together in the same
studio for many months, on the basis of what agreement I
don't know. Fittke had arrived from Munich with a technique which he liked and for a very short time Veruda tried it
out, on (I think) a single canvas. The influence of the older
painter (older than Fittke, that is) must have had an effect for
two reasons: first of all, Veruda spoke of Fittke's worth.
Through him, those of us who knew nothing about art
immediately felt respect for this very young painter. It is true
that Veruda later despaired of Fittke's future, thinking he
was too passive in the struggle for life and believing that he
would die of hunger if he did not take a job. Having known
Fittke for several years I always maintain Veruda was right.
The other reason why I think Veruda influenced Fittke was
that in the many years in which I knew him Fittke never
failed to stress his admiration for Veruda, who had died long
before. Perhaps this second reason loses its value, considering certain observations by your friend on the character of
Fittke, observations I agree with.

Dear Signor Del Conte, I thank you warmly for having got
me this study, which I will keep carefully, and I hope to see
you soon.

Yours ever

Ettore Schmitz.

In my family, love of music predominated. My brother
was becoming a concert player of standing. My sister Dora
loved singing and had a magnificent soprano voice. Her
husband, a very good violinist, was president of the Concert
Society and brought the most famous European concert

players who were passing through the city to our house. Ettore never played his violin in public since his technique was not very good, but in the family he enjoyed playing in a trio.

Understanding his need for isolation, I had a small studio built on a terrace beside our rooms, with a music-stand beside his desk and shelves for his favourite books. He, who never asked for anything, was immensely grateful for this idea of mine. He was delighted to have a refuge all to himself. But after *Senilità* he had definitely given up being a writer, and Italo Svevo was more and more cancelled out by Schmitz the businessman, who saw to the mixing of paints, guarded the valuable formulas, was involved in the administration of the firm, was trusted with particular tasks, and saw to contracts all over Europe. The hours of creative nostalgia were filled with music, with which he filled the solitude of his studio and hotel rooms.

I always travelled with my violin and when I got off in London they would look at me with respect at the station: Albert Hall, Wigmore Hall, or Queen's Hall? Whereas the car would take me to the furthest and coolest of the suburbs, where I delighted the neighbours with my playing.

However, despite his self-imposed restrictions, every now and then, in his tiny writing, he would sketch a play, put down a thought or an impression, or finalize a reflection on the back of an envelope or circular.

Though imprisoned in voluntary silence, his spirit continued to analyse life and examine people, whom he judged with a sharp yet indulgent eye, always finding extenuating circumstances for their sins. He never failed to help anyone and could do it with great tact. Even distant relatives always turned to him.

To me he confided all his doubts. It was only his finished work he seldom mentioned. Although he was the elder, he relied on me more and more with a touching, almost filial

trust. When he had to go to England, he would say: 'Either
you come with me, or I come with you.' In some things he
was like a child. He had no sense of the everyday necessities
of life and his amazing absent-mindedness became a legend
and an amusement to our many relations. He never carried
more than a single coin in his purse, because if he had had
two, he would have lost one of them.

Once, in Venice, during one of our many stays in the house
at Murano, beside the paint factory, we went into a chemist's
shop to buy two bottles of medicine. As we went out I said to
him: 'You take the medicines.' When we got home, I was
bewildered to see him take boxes and bottles of all sizes out of
his pockets. 'What's all this stuff?' I cried. 'Didn't you tell
me to take the medicines?' he said, naively. At nine in the
evening we had to send back to Zampironi the chemist, from
Murano to Venice, all the medicines they were impatiently
waiting for.

One day, when we were returning from Venice on the
steamer, I said to him, as we were preparing to disembark:
'Take the rug.' When we got on to the jetty I realized the rug
was very bulky. In it Ettore had wrapped the great table-
cloth from the boat.

Such incidents upset him but he managed to laugh at
himself in the end. Only once was he deeply upset, and the
result almost made him ill, for though he usually slept
soundly, he suffered from insomnia for a whole week. He had
left the office with a hundred and fifty lire to buy something
urgently needed at the factory, and had returned some hours
later without having found what he wanted but with a pretty
box of sweets in his hand and a hundred and sixty lire in his
wallet. It was impossible to know where either of these had
come from. Whenever it rained he lost an umbrella. I used to
buy him smart ones so that he would be sure to remember
them. One day he went out with a red-handled umbrella
which he lost. On another rainy day he went out with a grey
one and came home with the red one again! He was quite

capable of putting on two sets of cufflinks and then feeling some discomfort, an extra weight on his arms. One day he searched in vain for a red tie, and could not find it. When he came home, after a violent downpour, I saw that as he walked he was leaving a red trail behind him that looked to me like blood. Terrified, I pointed to his leg, and we found the tie twisted round his ankle. But his greatest moment of distractions was the time he forgot our little Letizia at the fair at Villacco.

One such distraction took place in Paris. He had gone into the Crédit Lyonnais. It was a drizzly day, I was waiting for him in a taxi outside, and it was a long time before he came out. At last he appeared looking very heated, pointed to a man who was moving away, and said: 'Do you see? That man's taken my umbrella. We were both leaning on the counter and suddenly he took it out of my hand and exclaimed: "Monsieur, c'est mon parapluie!" I said, "No, it's mine." He insisted so much that, in order to avoid a row, I let him take it.' 'Oh, what a shame!' I exclaimed indignantly. When we got back to the hotel, of course we found Ettore's umbrella in its usual place.

When he was old, he often told himself: 'I must be less absent-minded, so as not to lose my spectacles.' As he grew older, his absent-mindedness decreased, but what an effort it must have cost him to involve himself actively in the world of business and the factory! In his creative periods he actually withdrew from his surroundings, and his relationships with others became vague and fleeting. Through an act of will he withdrew from literature, which called him insistently, longingly. 'I remember that even before the grace which came to me through the whim of a great man,' he wrote, 'I always loved my literary demon. I did not repudiate it because I was upset at my lack of fame; I was afraid that it would stop me doing my duty, a duty I had imposed upon myself, towards my family and colleagues. It was a matter of honesty, because it was obvious that if I wrote a single line my work was ruined

for a whole week.' So for many years he did not write,
because a single line meant that he was less good at the work
he had daily to do. Distraction and reluctance entered into
him by stealth above all; he wanted to be an exemplary
worker.

Letizia was now entering adolescence. Ettore had opposed
my wish to have her educated at the convent of Notre Dame
de Sion, in accordance with the tradition of my very religious
family. He wanted her to go to state schools because he
believed they provided a more realistic approach, one better
adapted to living. Apart from this he left the responsibility
for Letizia's education entirely to me. In those years he was
too much absorbed in his work and his dreams to establish an
intimate and continuous relationship with his daughter.
Sometimes tiredness made him impatient, but when he
talked to her about serious matters, he did so without a trace
of authority, as a friend, and he taught her to face the
problems of life with unadorned sincerity. Even during her
happy childhood she had not been able to enjoy much of his
company. Periods of travel and holiday had been happy: at
the Lido in Venice, at Riccione, on long hikes in the
mountains and on the Carso, where we stayed at Sesano and
Prevallo. Once we walked for ten hours to reach the top of the
Mangart. The relationship between father and daughter then
became more intimate and enjoyable. Ettore wanted to take
her to the places where he had spent his own quiet
adolescence, the romantic landscapes along the Rhine and
the college of Segnitz near Würzburg: he also wanted to take
her to the little house in London. Letizia's resemblance to
her father, both physical and inner, grew more obvious: she
had the same bright eyes, the same high forehead, the same
thick eyebrows, the same smile, full of humanity, the same
freedom of spirit; and, temperamentally, she had the vein of
pessimism which was found in him. He watched her grow
freely and if he was sometimes severe he did not oppress her
with his personality. Letizia went to the classical high school

and was athletic. At twelve, she had bicycled as far as San Pietro del Carso; and she loved skating and tennis. Her life was joyous, full of the company of her Bliznakoff cousins, boys and girls, who lived in the house beside ours. I had managed to get her into Notre Dame de Sion for a single year, the year of her first communion. From me, Letizia had inherited a great love of order and a strong sense of duty. Study was easy for her, and she was attracted by the sciences rather than literature. She loved beautiful things and had good taste. After her marriage she became a collector, particularly of jewellery.

Our life went ahead harmoniously. Ettore seemed peaceful, but secretly his obsessions continued to gnaw at him. On 10 January 1906 he wrote in an album, the remaining pages of which are mostly empty:

Why the devil do I speak so much about my old age? Certainly not from fear of death, about which I feel neither curiosity nor fear. I think that in fact my life has been too short. It was full of dreams which I neither noted nor remember. I don't regret not having enjoyed enough, but I do sincerely regret not having caught and fixed so long a period of time. But then, suppose there were many others who felt as I do! Poor humanity! What a heap of autobiographies! Letizia grew up, and all I have of her early childhood is some pale photographs.

The things around me die, forgotten, every day because I look at them in a dream, bewildered by a world of people shrieking in my ear. A while ago Livia was twenty and now she is over thirty. I feel as if she has always been this age and that if I reach old age, we shall all have always been old.

He was forty-three and already felt his life was over. Whereas destiny still had many happy surprises in store for him.

The writer in him seemed fast asleep, almost unknown to us and apparently regarded by him with a sort of pity:

A few years ago, I remember a businessman broke into our
serious discussion and asked: 'Is it true that you are the
author of two novels?' I blushed, as an author does in these
circumstances and, as the businessman mattered to me, I
said: 'No, no, no! That was a brother of mine.' But that man,
I don't know why, wanted to meet the author of the two
novels, and spoke to my brother, who was not too pleased to
have something attributed to him which clearly impugned
his professional respectability.

A spark was needed to take him out of that half-sleep, and
this was found in a casual meeting with the Irish writer James
Joyce.

From the time of his first visit to England, Ettore had felt
the need to perfect his English. He knew German perfectly,
French fairly well (he had practised with me even at the time
of our engagement), but he knew only a little English.
Studying the language was the reason for his fortunate
friendship with Joyce, who had come to Trieste from Dublin
in the autumn of 1903, bringing with him his young wife,
Nora Barnacle. He was young, a little over twenty, he was
poor, and at the start of his marvellous literary career. A
tragi-comic adventure had befallen him on the way to
Trieste. He had taken the Vienna–Trieste train and had got
off by mistake at Ljubljana at four in the morning. When he
asked a passer-by next day for Via S. Nicolò, where the
Berlitz School in Trieste was, he realized he had got the
wrong city. And feeling very worried because he had little
money with him, he waited at Ljubljana station all day and
part of the night for the train to Trieste. When he arrived
there, he left his wife in the small park beside the station and
went to find the school and get some financial help. By
mistake he turned up in a street in the city where some
English sailors were quarrelling with some prostitutes. He
tried to act as interpreter and peacemaker, but was unsuccessful: when the police arrived he was arrested with the

others and kept in prison the whole day, while his poor wife waited for him sitting on a park bench, with no money and no knowledge of the language in that foreign city.

How often did I hear Joyce describing this adventure, the memory of which amused him enormously, with wild exuberance!

After teaching at the Berlitz School for a while, he left it and made a living from private English lessons, going from house to house. Ettore wanted not only to learn the language but to find an expert guide to modern English writing. He turned to Joyce, who at that time was a fashionable teacher of Trieste's rich bourgeoisie, and that was how they met.

Between the teacher who, however odd, was highly intelligent (he knew eighteen languages, ancient and modern), and his exceptional pupil, lessons developed in an unusual way. They had nothing to do with grammar; the pair of them talked of literature, and touched on a hundred other subjects. Even I took part in them. The expressions Joyce used were extremely amusing and he spoke, like us, in Trieste dialect; indeed, he spoke in a working-class dialect which he had learned in the dark streets of the city where he loved to spend time. Even in Switzerland and in Paris the family still spoke in this dialect, including the children, who had been born in Trieste – Giorgio, who had inherited his father's fine voice, and Lucia, who became a dancer and a very talented designer. I still remember her magnificent illustrations for a poem by Chaucer on the Virgin Mary.

Despite the differences of age and nationality, friendship immediately arose between the two men. Joyce, who had never spoken of his literary work to anyone before, soon brought his manuscripts to Villa Veneziani. There were the poems in *Chamber Music* and some chapters of *Dubliners*. I remember going down to the garden after the story 'The Dead', the last chapter of *Dubliners*, had been read, to pick some flowers and give them to the author to express my admiration. My husband in his turn gave Joyce the two forgotten volumes, first *A Life*, for which he had a special affection, and then *As a Man Grows Older*, as if to say: 'I too was once a writer.' Joyce read them at once and during the next lesson said he felt Svevo had been unjustly neglected. He added warmly that some pages of *As a Man Grows Older* could not have been better done by the great masters of the French novel. These unexpected words were a balm to Ettore's heart. He gazed wide-eyed at Joyce, delighted and amazed. Never had he thought to hear such praise of his forgotten novels. That day he could not leave Joyce, he accompanied him all the way back to his home in Piazza Vico, telling him about his literary disappointments. It was the first time he had opened his heart to anyone and showed his profound bitterness.

Joyce spoke widely of his discovery of Ettore to those he knew; particularly to the intellectuals who predominated among them. He even recited the last pages of *As a Man Grows Older* by heart, and raged against the critics' blindness, maintaining that Svevo was a highly original novelist, the only modern Italian writer who interested him. But despite such praises, the people of Trieste remained deaf and incredulous.

In Ettore, Joyce found a mentality similar to his own, an analytical method he found congenial. In a lecture given in Paris in 1937, Louis Gillet even said that Joyce had been influenced by only two Italian writers, Giambattista Vico and Italo Svevo.

From then on, during their lessons, they spoke constantly of literary plans and problems. Ettore confided to Joyce that he was planning to write a story about an old man and a girl – later written under the title 'La Novella del Buon Vecchio e della Bella Fanciulla' ('The Story of the Nice Old Man and the Pretty Girl') – and Joyce discussed with him in detail the concept of Bloom which was later developed in *Ulysses*.

On the unconfident Ettore, the Irishman's combative, tenacious character and well-rooted confidence (as a young man he had said to an elderly poet: 'I admit that you have had no influence whatever on me, but it is deplorable that you are too old to feel mine') had a good effect. It can be seen even in the description of Joyce which Ettore gave to a meeting held by the *Convegno*[1] in Milan on 8 March 1927:

> He is over forty. Lean, lithe, tall, he might almost seem a sportsman if he had not the negligent gait of a person who does not care what he does with his limbs.
>
> I believe I am right in thinking that those limbs have been very much neglected and that they have never known either sport or gymnastics. What I mean is that from near he does not give the impression of being the tough fighter that his courageous work would lead you to expect. He is very shortsighted and wears strong glasses that make his eyes look enlarged. Those eyes are blue and very notable even without the glasses, and they gaze with a look of ceaseless curiosity matched with supreme coldness. I cannot help imagining that Joyce's eye would rest no less curiously and no less coldly on any adversary with whom he might have an encounter.[2]

Joyce's admiration and agreement were a miraculous balm to the deep wound which Ettore's self-esteem had suffered, a wound still tender and burning; and it was only then that he ceased to look upon his novels as youthful mistakes. Unrecognized, his talent had remained buried under what he called the 'sadness of silence'. And now, here was a friend who awoke the writer in him, this time for good.

The Great War separated them. Joyce took refuge in Zürich, and then moved to Paris. He did not return to Trieste, but he was to reappear in Svevo's life and to assume a very important role in it.

1. *Il Convegno* was an avant-garde literary periodical in Milan which ran its own literary circle.

2. From *James Joyce* by Italo Svevo, translated by Stanislaus Joyce (New Directions, New York, 1950). See Appendix, pp. 147ff.

WITH THE OUTBREAK OF WAR, or more precisely, with Italy's entry into it, our large family was scattered about Europe. The big house was left empty. My parents, who had Italian citizenship, took refuge in England. My sister Dora settled in Florence, Nella and Fausta chose Zürich; even our only child Letizia wanted to leave us to follow the fortunes of her fiancé, Antonio Fonda, a young Istrian who had volunteered for the Italian army. She went to live with her aunt in Florence. We all had the illusion that victory, which was certain, would bring Italy to Trieste in a few months.

We stayed on alone in the city to see to the interests of the firm. Our life underwent a profound change. Frenzied activity was followed by calm, silence, and anxious waiting. The factory was no longer working. In a few days a storm had suddenly overwhelmed the atmosphere of our life. In August 1915, Austrian military experts and technicians arrived at the factory to take over the plant and materials; they also wanted the jealously-guarded secret of the paint formula, and threatened Ettore with internment. Quickly he thought up a trick. At night, with desperate urgency, helped by an elderly workman linked to the family by ties of long-term loyalty and who was very devoted to Ettore – who knew how to make humble people love him – the special material was locked up in a little room. Next day fake formulas were solemnly handed over to the military commission. These were tried out, with results that can be imagined, in the factory set up to forward the Austrian war effort at Pola della Imperiale and Regia Marina. Ettore was always delighted with this trick, which was only one of the many – now part of the city's folklore – practised on the Austrian authorities by the people of Trieste. As a reprisal, the Austrians stripped the factory. Nine trucks of machines and raw materials were stolen and taken to the stronghold at Pola.

Suddenly Ettore found himself in a silent house, without further worries, without responsibilities. We were alone in the big villa, and he could now dedicate himself, as he had never done before, uninterruptedly, to studying the violin. Even our friends had scattered: many had crossed the Italian frontier, others had been sent to concentration camps set up in distant parts of Austria. Every evening we met like conspirators, the few who were left, at the Caffè del Tergesteo: the Luzzattos, the Vidalis, the Danielis, to swap news, illusions and hopes. Joyce was in Zürich, Silvio Benco interned, the journalists Giulio Cesari and Riccardo Zampieri were languishing among political deportees in an Austrian castle. An obscure threat hung over Ettore too. His name was in the political black book, and he was continually watched because he had taken part in the city's struggle when its nationality was threatened. As a young man he had, as I have said, been a constant contributor to the *Indipendente*, a rebel paper, and with other willing youngsters he had offered to edit it to avoid its suspension when the Austrian police arrested the staff and threatened its future. In 1895 he had helped carry the bier at the funeral, which was also a demonstration, of an irredentist journalist who had died of an illness caught in an Austrian prison: Enrico Juretig, from Gorizia. When he was only twenty-five Ettore already held positions of command in the ardent irredentist movement in Trieste, in the Lega Nazionale and in the Società Ginnastica. A friend of the most representative supporters of Italy in Trieste, the learned Attilio Hortis and the poet Riccardo Pitteri, head of the Lega Nazionale, he had always, without deviating or wavering, been an Italian. Whenever there was an election, he had always returned to Trieste to give his vote to the Italian cause, whatever part of Europe he might find himself in.

Equally, the Veneziani family was more than ever suspect. The Austrian police had put a black mark against the name of Edoardo Veneziani, my father's brother, colleague of Oberdan, outstanding agitator and conspirator, who had been expelled from Austria. Another two brothers of his,

Carlo and Enrico, had been followers of Garibaldi, the first wounded in 1860 in the campaign in Sicily, the second having been in the campaign of 1867 in the plain around Rome. Other much-hated names were those of Felice Venezian, a cousin of my father's, the animator and leader of the movement for national union between Trieste and Istria; and Giacomo Venezian, who at the age of fifty-four had volunteered for the war of redemption, thus continuing a family tradition, because another Giacomo Venezian died at the age of eighteen in 1849 fighting with Garibaldi at Vascello, as colour-sergeant in the Medical Corps.

Ettore's long periods abroad had not made him at all cosmopolitan. He always remained proudly Triestian and Italian. So he was often called to the central office of the Austrian police in Via Caserma. Sometimes he was abruptly woken in the middle of the night, so that his frail nerves might break under the hammer-blows of an interrogation. All this he bore calmly, strong in his faith. Although he was not of a polemical temperament, he knew how to answer the oppressors with smiling irony and quiet defiance.

Once an official of Slav origin asked slyly: 'Is it true that you belonged to the Lega Nazionale?' 'Certainly,' Ettore replied. 'How was that?' the man asked threateningly. 'And what about you, did you belong to the society of S S Cyril and Methodius?' 'Yes.' 'Well, that's the same thing,' Ettore concluded, with the greatest calm, staring straight at the man, who was silenced.

In this atmosphere, life continued. A leaden pall seemed to hang over us as we waited for the occasional rare letter from our distant loved ones, which my sisters Nella and Fausta tried to forward from Switzerland. Ettore wrote to Letizia, now separated from us by a barrier of fire:

My dearest daughter, you're in a great hurry to age me. It's now the 10th and I shall be fifty-four only on the 19th. I protest. It's true that these war years are each worth twice their length. Thank you a thousand times for your good wishes. The best thing to wish for would be for this time to be over – it's too long already. Do you remember how you left, after a discussion which lasted only a few minutes? It seemed like leaving for a holiday, whereas you left for a really long stretch. I no longer make up fairy-tales, reality distracts me too much from dreams . . . if I may put it so. I'm becoming a very serious businessman. My father used to tell me I'd become wise at forty. So I'm fourteen years late. I hope this precocity isn't hereditary, for your sake. Until a couple of weeks ago, I used to play the violin every day. Then came some new thoughts, nothing serious, just business matters which won't go away and I must face, and I gave up playing the violin too. Today I went to look at it. It has taken advantage of the rest to free itself from all four strings, which had been played out. Nothing sadder than an unstrung stringed instrument. You'll understand when I say that the corpse of an animal, though sad, is more vital and complete. And then there's the sad fact that new strings can be found only several kilometres away from here and have to be fetched through a sea of mud. I'll make up my mind this evening. This time I also looked at your violin to see if it could help me. The mice must have eaten it, because it's no longer around. I put the bow away safely. You see how careful and tidy I am. Kindest greetings to all our dear ones. A loving embrace

from your Papa.

The roar of cannon was close: overhead aeroplanes brought the tricolour wings of our country into the sky now and then.

Ettore was deep in literature. Under the influence of Joyce his tastes had taken a new direction. Joyce, who was in love with Swift, had made him read all his works; and Ettore spent whole nights reading Green's history of English literature.[1] He played the violin a great deal. At the start he

1. Probably J. R. Green's widely read *A Short History of the English People*.

had refused to embark on any creative work, then he began to
collect his thoughts on many small sheets of paper, for a book
of memoirs which was never completed. They were separate
notes, one memory recalling another, with a link between
them, though it was often broken.

13.6.17

An old man has to be tidy. Now, at the age of fifty-seven, I
have to use three sorts of glasses, and that has given me a
habit of tidiness. So I'm beginning my book of reminiscences
again and am confident I can carry it through. So many things
and people who were dear to me will die completely, and I
regret this immensely. How pale those things and people are!
They are merely abstract ideas and perhaps false ones. I
myself will end up believing that I've always been as I am
today, while remembering hatreds and loves I no longer
have. All the same I suspect that, in changing desires, we
don't really change essentially. Perhaps what matters is the
way we do it. But, having recorded too little, I cannot check
that. Certainly I remember violent desires and violent revul-
sions, but I no longer know whether the things I loved
escaped me because of inertia or through fate, or if the things
I hated stayed with me because I was too unprotected or
because they were too strong. Napoleon must have known
his own life much better, even though he wrote it down only
when his real life was over. Four years ago, before the Great
War, I undertook a long journey all over Europe. I remember
that as I passed them I wished all the fields to bear fruit and
hoped the peasants, who were dressed in all kinds of clothes,
should have the due results of their labours. And I felt I had
done a great thing and that Napoleon might have envied me.
Then, when the war broke out, I suffered over every defeat; I
certainly had no need of war to free me from hatred.

The war touched us in a particularly tragic way. On the
night of 4 December 1917, a night of terrible winds, we heard
a fearful explosion opposite Villa Veneziani. It was a torpedo
fired by Luigi Rizzo hitting the jetty instead of the battleship

74   *Budapest.*[1] The terrifying blast was followed by voices shrieking wildly for about ten minutes, and then by a tragic silence:
it was the sailors of the *Wien* drowning in the storm. Ettore,
deeply stricken and deeply human as he was, in spite of the
strict blackout, immediately ordered the powerful lights in
the garden to be lit, to give the shipwrecked men the comfort
of light and some guidance in the stormy night. Eighteen
sailors, bewildered, half-naked, sodden, took refuge in the
porter's lodge. They were all from the coast of Istria and in
our dialect they cursed the officers who were amusing themselves in the city's big hotels that night. Ettore's provident
action to help them lasted all night. He was very sensitive to
the sufferings of every creature and felt strongly involved.

In response to these feelings, and influenced by the books
of Schücking and Fried,[2] he set out, in those years of
suffering, to write a humanitarian work, a plan for universal
peace. Whether he finished it, or whether he partly destroyed
it, I do not know. Only a few extracts from it remained
among his unpublished work. Probably he thought it a
chimera later on, since the book on Zeno ends thus: 'There
will be a tremendous explosion, but no one will hear and the
earth will return to its nebulous state and go wandering
through the sky, free at last from parasites and disease.'

In 1918, in collaboration with a nephew of his, Aurelio
Finzi, he began a translation of a work by Freud, *On Dreams.*
Ettore's discovery of Freud was a great event for him, and he
remained steeped in him for the rest of his life. He himself
liked to tell how, in about 1910, he had approached him:

A neurotic friend of mine went to Vienna to undergo treatment; the only good that came out of it was the warning it

1. Luigi Rizzo was the lieutenant in charge of a raid in which two small
torpedo-boats attacked two battleships at point-blank range after breaking through the harbour defences.
2. Walther Schücking and Alfred Fried were pacifist writers who
published numerous works on international diplomacy, including the
post First World War peace settlement.

gave to me. He had himself psychoanalysed and returned from the cure destroyed, as lacking in will-power as before, but with his feebleness aggravated by the conviction that, being as he was, he could not behave otherwise. It was he who convinced me how dangerous it was to explain to a man how he is made, and every time I see him I love him for the sake of our old friendship, but also with this new gratitude.

Psychoanalysis, as I said, was never forgotten by him. It sharpened his psychological insights, but had only a secondary effect upon his work. It is not true, as has been said, that he himself underwent psychoanalysis. He confessed that he had made some psychoanalytical tests on himself, which contradicted Freud's theories: perhaps the same tests made by his character Zeno to free himself from his passion for smoking.

The war years would have passed in wearisome monotony if Ettore's inner life had not illuminated them. The factory had been reopened and was working at a reduced pace under the control of an imperial commissar, who also administered the finances. Ettore had protested against the takeover and the non-payment of invoices and had won his case. The house was occupied by the families of Austrian officers and we lived isolated in our own apartment, with the nightmare of their presence. Ettore felt Letizia's absence acutely. Other members of his family were far away too: his sisters, married to Italian citizens, were living in Florence and Milan; his brother Ottavio had been in Vienna for many years. The tragic death of a nephew, Ortensia's son Umbertino, had affected him deeply, and other relatives had died as well, not tragically, but suddenly. On 13 August 1918 my brother-in-law Adolfo died of heart disease in our house, where he had come to seek relief from his sufferings, only a few weeks before the liberation we had longed for so ardently. As he was dying, Ettore comforted him with a compassionate lie, telling him that the Italian army had occupied Udine. 'Too late for me, too late,' sighed the dying man, who throughout his life had been the purest of patriots. All these many misfortunes had helped to make Ettore pessimistic, almost resigned to the harshest blows of fate. He always expected the worst, and was prepared to meet suffering at any moment, almost as if in the deepest part of his being he had foreseen the appalling suffering the Second World War was to bring to his beloved daughter.

On 30 October 1918, the day of the Trieste uprising, in spite of having Austrians billeted in the house, at about midday we raised the tricolour flag above the villa. For three years we had kept it in a secret hiding-place. In the preceding week Ettore had taken an energetic part in the preparatory meetings of the deputy Edoardo Gasser. Staying in our villa was the sister of Field-Marshal von Cicerich who, when she arrived in the garden and saw the enemy flag fluttering proudly in the wind, turned very pale. My husband went up to her politely and with a touch of irony said: 'Cheer up, madam. Even in the shadow of the tricolour you will sleep well.' He was appointed a member of the Committee of Public Safety and, as always, played his part in the city with the spirit of a true irredentist.

At the end of November we left for Florence to embrace our daughter Letizia once again, after three years apart. We were so impatient that we made the journey to Venice by sea, in spite of the danger of mines, and found Letizia pale and unwell, just convalescent from the Spanish flu. The girl had become a woman, matured by nearly three years of anxieties and troubles. We also met Tony Fonda, her fiancé, who had fought on the Carso and in the Veneto, and at the age of twenty had been promoted to captain. Our meetings and tales were never-ending. Ettore wanted to make a short trip to Milan to see his nephews, the children of his sister Paola. We all went back to Trieste together and in the first Christmas of peace celebrated Letizia's engagement.

With the war over, Olga Veneziani's large family scattered

about Europe gradually came together again. My parents had
returned from London, my sisters from Florence and
Zürich, my nephew from Bulgaria. The young girls had
become women, the boys had suffered and fought. Those
were emotional days. The rhythm of business had increased,
but Ettore now devoted himself to literature. When his
friend Giulio Cesari returned from the concentration camp,
Ettore urged him to set up the first large national newspaper
in Trieste, and Cesari brought out *La Nazione*. Ettore agreed
to write for it, promising to specialize in politics; but his pen
betrayed him: he wrote eight little articles and a satire, which
instead were literature, and continued with a series of long
impressions of London, thus establishing his first contact
with the public, which had not yet recognized him.

On 24 April 1919 the wedding of Letizia and Captain
Antonio Fonda was celebrated, very simply. They then came
to live with us, bringing a breath of life into the silent house.
In June 1920 their first son, Piero, was born. My husband,
whose family affections were very tender, was much affected
to find himself a grandfather. He was then fifty-nine. Our
son-in-law's entry into the firm lightened his work a great
deal. Ettore had been working on his new novel for some
time, and in July 1922, when we went to spend the summer at
Poggioreale, in the Carso, he was able to give his full
attention to the definitive version of *The Confessions of Zeno*.
He would shut himself up in the sitting-room for the whole
day, and type. No one interrupted or disturbed him. He
smoked a great deal. When he came out he was totally
absorbed, almost absent. He never spoke about the work he
had finished. Sometimes, but seldom, he took it up again at
night. He would interrupt it by going for short walks in the
pine woods with his grandson Piero. He was very fond of
children, watching them intensely and attentively, and able
to draw the hidden, profound meaning from every curious
expression of theirs, every instinctive movement. From these
contacts he drew treasures which are found in some of his still

unpublished stories. He told how Paolo, Letizia's second son, seeing two carabinieri one day in full dress, splendid and befeathered, asked him anxiously: 'Grandpa, do the carabinieri know we aren't thieves?'

Having written *Zeno*, Ettore immediately sensed that the work he had finished, which had taken three years, was good. Gradually, as he corrected it, he threw away the previous drafts. I think he let no one read what was unpublished. He had jotted down the first draft in a fortnight in 1919, after the articles in *La Nazione*. As the ghosts took shape, his contributions to the paper became fewer. He was surprised by the force of inspiration, which gave him no peace.

If Italy hadn't come to me, I'm sure I'd never have imagined I could write my novel four months after the arrival of our troops, as if it were quite natural at the age of fifty-eight. With the arrogance of the 'liberated' I seemed suddenly to have acquired the rights of a citizen for myself and for my 'little tongue'.

The ardent enthusiasm which had filled the hearts of all irredentists in the excitement of liberty had at once been changed in him – despite his deep-seated fears over his difficulties of expression – into a great creative force. But he was well aware that his style could not be decorated with words he did not feel, words which did not belong to his living language, and that his living language was the dialect of Trieste.

The book was published at his own expense in 1923 by the firm of Cappelli.[1] The Italian critics barely mentioned it. Those in Trieste, Silvio Benco, Ferdinando Pasini and Donatello D'Orazio, praised it in the local press; but Ettore was hurt by his lack of success in the rest of Italy, as even his health showed. He became melancholy, and his heart troubles grew worse. He wrote:

1. Licinio Cappelli, from Bologna, had opened a bookshop in Trieste after the war and published many Triestine authors.

Well, I laugh when my critics, since they cannot call me a great writer, out of kindness call me a great financier and manufacturer. I am neither one nor the other. I was never in the higher reaches of finance, and as a manufacturer I was useful to my firm because I kept very busy; this was the result of an iron resolve, supported by strong gratitude for the relative independence and well-being which industry allowed me.

However, in 1925, unexpectedly and suddenly, the sun rose gloriously and lit up his life. He was then sixty-three. I remember that day in January. We were sitting round the big table where we had our meals with Letizia's family – she now had three children. Ettore absent-mindedly opened a letter from Paris. He began reading it aloud and even the way he was addressed took his breath away. It began: 'Dear Sir, dear Master', and was a letter of praise and congratulation from Valery Larbaud. I do not remember ever having seen Ettore so radiant. It was to James Joyce, who had reappeared like a kindly star in his sky, that he owed this great satisfaction. After the war, in 1919, Joyce and Ettore had met in Paris, and whenever Ettore was passing through he would go to the Place Robiac, where he was always welcomed as an old friend. Joyce always kept a vivid memory of Trieste, and would have liked to return there to live. Ettore took him the notes for the last episode of *Ulysses*, which he had left in our care. They consisted of a jumble of papers which filled an entire suitcase. This is the odd, original letter in which Joyce asked Ettore for a special favour:

'Boulevard Raspail 5, Paris VII. 5 January 1921
'Dear Mr Schmitz, the Circe episode was finished some time ago, but four typists refused to copy it. At last a fifth one turned up, but she works very slowly, so the work will not be ready until the end of this month. They tell me it will come to 170 pages of commercial-sized paper. The episode of Aeneas, which is nearly finished, will also be ready around the end of

the month. According to a plan prepared by my lawyer in New York *Ulysses* will come out around 15 June in a private and limited edition of 1500 copies, of which 750 will be for Europe. The price will be £6 a copy. I foresee £1,000 as a down payment. At the same time articles and handouts will be prepared to capture the castle, with what result I don't know and care very little.

'Now for the important thing: I cannot move from here (as I thought I could) before May. In fact for months and months I haven't got to bed before two or three in the morning, working without a break. Soon I shall have exhausted the notes I brought with me here to write these two episodes. In Trieste, in the district where my brother-in-law lives, there is a flat marked Via Sanità 2, and on the third floor of the said building, in the bedroom at present occupied by my brother, at the back of the building overlooking the house of public insecurity (police station), there is an oilcloth brief-case fastened with a rubber band the colour of a nun's belly and measuring approximately 95 cm by 70 cm. In this brief-case I placed the written symbols of the flashes which sometimes flickered languidly across my soul.

'The weight is estimated at 4.78 kg. Having urgent need of these notes for the last part of my literary work entitled *Ulysses* or *On the Greek Sea*, I am turning to you, my most esteemed colleague, asking you to let me know if anyone from your family is proposing to come to Paris soon, in which case I shall be extremely grateful if that person would have the kindness to bring me the brief-case I have mentioned.

'Therefore, dear Signor Schmitz, if any of your family should be travelling in this direction it would be the greatest boon to me if they could bring that bundle, which is not remotely heavy since, you will understand, it is full of papers that I have covered in my fairest hand with a pen, or sometimes with pencil (*Bleistift*) when there was no pen handy. But whatever you do, don't break the elastic band, or it will all be in a mess. The best thing would be to take plenty

of those traps (*sic*) for sale at Greinitz and Nephews [hard-
ware store] near the "Piccolo", in Piazza Goldoni, and my
brother,[1] who is professor at the *Berlitz Cul*, will pay. At all
events send us a couple of lines – how we eat them up!
Revoltella have written to me saying that there are boys to
examine at five soldi apiece, after which they become doctors
of the revoltella [i.e. revolver], and that I should come there
and give them their exercise (*Aufgabe*) for five soldi, but I
have not replied because it is all stupid nonsense, and anyway
the postage stamp, plus the paper, would cost me three soldi
at present rates, so that would leave two soldi for train-fares
and food and drink for three days and all that.

'Cordial greetings and forgive me if my small brain
sometimes plays me up a bit. Please write soon, I beg you.

'James Joyce.'

This letter shows the cordial relations which existed
between the two writers, from which arose their close understanding in time of trouble. Ettore's bitterness at the hostility
with which he believed *Zeno* was surrounded and his own
rebellious feelings about this had been expressed to his
already famous friend, to whom he sent a copy of the book.
He had no confidence that he would be heard; his pessimistic
temperament forbade him to hope. In those days, too, after
their first friendly meeting, the relationship between the two
had been limited to short visits when we were passing
through Paris and the exchange of affectionate greetings on
new year cards. But Joyce in his triumphant advance had
heard his friend's bitter cry and answered it.

'30 January 1924

'Dear Friend,

'I went to the station but no train was coming (not even
late) at the hour you had told me; I was sorry for that. When
will you come through Paris again? Could you not spend the
night?

1. Stanislaus Joyce.

'Thanks for the novel with its inscription. I have two copies, having ordered one from Trieste. I am reading it with great pleasure. Why are you so desperate? You must know that it is by far your best book. As far as the Italian critics are concerned, I don't know. But have review copies sent to M. Valery Larbaud, M. Benjamin Crémieux, Mr T. S. Eliot, Mr F. M. Ford.

'I shall speak with or write to these literary men about it. I may write again when I have finished. For the present, two things interest me. The theme: I should never have thought that smoking could dominate a person in that way; secondly, the treatment of time in the novel. You certainly do not lack sharpness and I see that the last-but-one line of *Senilità*, "Sí! Angiolina pensa e piane, etc.", has impressively developed in privacy.

'P.S . Send it also to Gilbert Seldes, *The Dial*, New York.'

Following his advice, Ettore hastened to send the book to Larbaud and Crémieux. The result was the letter of unexpected praise.

'11 January 1925
'Dear Sir, Dear Master ["Egregio Signore e Maestro"],

'Since I received and read *La Coscienza di Zeno*, I have done all I can to make this admirable book known in France. Propaganda by word of mouth only, but efficacious, as you will see.

'Last summer, the review *Commerce* was founded, to appear every three months, edited by the greatest of our poets, Paul Valéry, by Léon-Paul Fargue, known by the élite as one of the best writers of the avant-garde, and by me; and this review immediately went into the front rank of French literary reviews. The idea for this publication came from the Princess di Bassiano, wife of Prince Roffredo Caetani, of Rome, who has provided us with funds and also gives us useful advice.

'Before the review was founded I gave the Princess *La*

Coscienza di Zeno to read and now that we are preparing nos IV and V of the review, she would like us to publish some extracts from it, between 10 and 15 pages. There is no difficulty about translation: among our best avant-garde writers there are three or four excellent translators of Italian, ready to work on the pages we choose. The only thing missing, therefore, is your authorization and that of the publisher Cappelli.

'For my part, I should like to write a short study of your work in *Commerce*, a study I should later give in a more complete form to the *Nouvelle Revue Française* or the *Revue Européenne*. But I do not know your other books, which last summer I tried without success to find in Bologna and Florence, and I should be very grateful if you would be so good as to send them to me.

'Our friend James Joyce, as you will have heard, has had to undergo another operation on his eyes, but is now well and working.

'Please forgive so many questions and believe me, dear sir, dear Master, your devoted admirer,

'Valery Larbaud.'

Nervously, Ettore at once sent him *As a Man Grows Older* and *A Life*. After reading the two books Larbaud wrote:

'10 February 1925

'Dear Sir, Dear Master,

'I received your letter of the 16th. Forgive me for not having answered sooner. I have been very busy. Thank you for the books.

'As far as the matter I wrote to you about goes, we are organizing the campaign in your favour. Perhaps we shall start with an article, by one of us, in an Italian paper this summer.

'Then, for the fifth number of *Commerce*, which will appear next October, we shall prepare a selection of pages translated into French. From *Senilità* we shall take pages

162–172, which I have read to several friends and which were received enthusiastically; someone mentioned the name of Marcel Proust.

'From *La Coscienza di Zeno* we shall take pages 16–32 and 477–496. From *Una Vita*, which a friend of mine is now reading, I don't yet know whether we shall take an example. Perhaps we may make changes in this choice, and perhaps we shall also give titles (but in brackets) to the pages chosen. The title *Senilità* seems to us not very suitable for the novel, and if it were all to be translated into French, I think it would be better to call it *Emilio Brentani*. We are impatient to start the campaign, but every one of us has so much to do that things cannot go as fast as we should like them to; but your name is already known among the best young writers here. The rest will come gradually.

'Believe me, dear Master, your most devoted admirer,
    'Valery Larbaud.'

I still keep Ettore's reply to these letters, one of the few from that period which have remained among his papers.

. . . If you knew what a revolution your two letters have made in my life. I have re-read *Senilità* and I am now seeing the book that I was resigned to regarding as worthless in the light of the judgement you have made of it; I have also re-read *Una Vita*. James Joyce always said that there is only ever room for one novel in a man's heart (by then he had not even begun *Ulysses*) and that when one writes several it is always the same one disguised in other words. But in that case my one novel must be *Una Vita*. Only it is so ill-written (much worse than the two others) that I would need to redo it. And for such a task I am not sure I have either the time or the health.

All the same it has given me a more intense feeling of my life and my past.

I am also engaged in other kinds of reading. I have got hold of *À la recherche du temps perdu* by Proust. It has been interesting for me to get up to date with your literature. You know that during the war we in Trieste were outside the circle of civilization, and perhaps that is why the last name that reached me from your country is that of Anatole France. But I also have the impression that in Italy in general we study what you produce less than we did in the past. In my youth I believe that a book published in Paris would have been in our hands within hours. Now it is the Goncourt prize-winners (*Rabevel*[1] for example) who succeed. The objections people make to Proust could not prevent his winning readers. At bottom they are the same objections which potentially could have injured Zola. But he had the good fortune to find a critic in Italy of the force and reputation of Francesco de Sanctis. Monsieur Borgese[2] said recently that he wanted to give up criticism so as to be able to get on with his own work. Perhaps one of these days . . .

Meanwhile, in the spring of 1925, taking advantage of one of our business trips to London, we stopped in Paris to meet the two illustrious literary men who had taken such a lively interest in the Svevo case. Joyce arranged a dinner in a restaurant near the Gare Montparnasse. A young French writer, Nino Frank, was also there. Ettore, who as a rule was sociable, friendly and sweet-tempered with everyone, at once found himself perfectly attuned to his new friends, who showed an admiration which astonished him. Seized by what seemed like a slight intoxication, he talked a great deal that evening. He loved to be listened to, all the more when those he was speaking to were like himself.

Next evening, we were invited to one of the most aristocratic literary salons, that of Princess Bassiano Caetani, the patroness of *Commerce*, at her house in Versailles, the Villa Romana. Larbaud and Crémieux were there too. During the long, brilliant conversation my husband mentioned a new novel he was working on. This must have been the one later entitled *Short Sentimental Journey*.

1. Lucien Fabre's *Rabevel ou le Mal des Ardents*, Paris, 1923.
2. Giuseppe Borgese, a critic who wrote in *Corriere della Sera*.

During that remarkable and happy stay we also met Crémieux's wife, a woman of profound, sensitive intelligence. She was Corsican by birth, had studied in Florence, and spoke Italian perfectly, with a perfect accent. We met every day, either in her drawing-room or for lunch here and there. The lively sympathy between her and Ettore very soon became friendship, and a correspondence began between them which ended only at his death. To her he confided feelings which he liked to hide from others and, always unsure of himself, he drew strength and comfort from her friendly presence.

From Paris we went on to London, where Ettore received the following letter from Larbaud, who was getting ready for the translation of some chapters of *As a Man Grows Older*.

'Valbois par Saint Pourçain-sur-Sioule (Allier)
'24 June 1925

'Dear Sir,

'You speak and write French so well that I would be ashamed to write to you in Italian. I have just received your letter from London. I shall not be in Paris when you are passing through and I regret it greatly. I am very behindhand with my work and that is why I have decided to immure myself in a very isolated house in the country. My holidays begin at the end of next month, and I plan to go first to Genoa, then to the isle of Elba, but I don't know how long I shall stay there nor what I shall do after that. Ah! If I could only go to Trieste. Perhaps . . .

'Here are the two Venetian (?) expressions that bother me and that I would be very grateful if you could explain – though perhaps it will be best to leave them as they are in my translation – but I want to know their exact meaning.

'It's at the end of p. 167:

'He suffered when, hesitating, she hid her hands in her hair, with a masculine gesture, or out of surprise cried

"O, *la balena!*" – or when, seeing him sad, she asked
him: "Are you *invelenao* today?"[1]

'I think I can guess at the second; it is the first that is difficult. And what French equivalent could there be? I would like – but give me your opinion, and I will go along with it – to leave the two expressions as they are and explain them in a note.

'I am about to work on the translation of *Ulysses* – which is part (and a sizeable part) of my work overdue. By the time I leave here the first 200 pages or so will be ready – and the passage from *Senilità* also.

'Au revoir, dear Sir; it has been a great pleasure to make your acquaintance, and I shall really do my very best to get to Trieste to pay you a proper visit. Please give my best respects to Madame Schmitz and believe me,

'Your admirer and devoted translator
'V. Larbaud.'

Full of gratitude, Ettore replied at once:

London, 26 June 1929
Dear M. Larbaud,

I have your very kind letter of the 24th. I am glad you wrote to me in French because your writing seems to me more authentic that way. I too know the gloomy doubts which come to one when writing in a foreign language. The last letter I wrote to you was in French. I was then reading French books and to my great chagrin realized I had put in too many accents. I rushed to the post to get my letter back but it had already gone.

O, La balena. When you told me that a certain word was giving you difficulty I immediately thought of that formidable and all too defenceless cetacean (yes, it is he) that can be

1. This sentence, in the first and second editions of the book, was omitted in the English-language translation (Putnam & Company Ltd, London, 1932).

invoked when one is amazed by the sight of something huge. Not being sure whether I could get a letter to you directly, I wrote to M. Crémieux asking him to hand on my explanation to you, or else to wait for you to return to Paris and then tell you about it.

The difficulty is that I have realized that the word is not used nowadays, even in Venice. But I had it from a Venetian speaker. Shortly before I wrote *Senilità* I went to Venice for a few days, which I spent in the company of some Venetian painters. The whale swam from mouth to mouth. But I now think that the only Italian who uses it is myself. This is a nuisance, but it is the kind of thing you may find on re-reading a book written thirty years ago, and involving a Venetian word, at that.

Venetian is spoken by only 240,000 people (the other Venetians don't speak it) and is a lively, fresh language unrestricted by academics or dictionaries. The language comes and goes in a small area lived in by a people which is sentimental, happy and sharp-tongued, and therefore needs a great many words, and I bet Venetians will claim that the whale has never passed through the lagoon.

Invelenao! A Triestino, who is in fact a Venetian, would not use this word for *avvelenato* (poisoned), nor would he even use it in the sense of irritated or cross, as everyone in Venice does. I have no idea how those two words can be translated and I leave myself trustfully in your hands.

I shall be leaving here in a week and will stop in Paris for two or three days. Then I go to Gleichenberg (Austria) for a three-week cure which I need urgently. In the second half of August I shall be in Trieste. I shall be happy if you decide to come and see us. I have already made a programme of the things I will show you and which I am certain you'll like, because I'm sure that I now know you better than you think I do.

My wife thanks you for your courteous greetings and asks to be remembered to you.

I don't know how to express my gratitude for what you are doing for me and for my poor affairs. I see you all alone with

the old book, to which you are giving life and light, sacrific-
ing the time which must be so precious for your own work.
Thank you.
    Yours devotedly
      Ettore Schmitz.

We went back to Trieste feeling happy, enriched by so
many new things.

And there, although involved in the usual rhythm of Trieste,
Ettore's heart was still in Paris. To Madame Crémieux he
wrote:

                    Villa Veneziani, Trieste 10
                       28 November 1925
Dear Friend,

    Your kind letter of the 21st aroused my usual feeling of
gratitude. In these last days I had to write to Joyce, who told
me (poor soul) that he had to undergo an operation on his
eyes for the seventh time, and telling him what was happen-
ing to me, I said that for advice I had turned to the very kind
Madame Crémieux, the only Parisian who had the postal
service at her disposal every day.

    Perfectly reassured by what you said, I did what you
suggested at once and accepted Prezzolini's[1] suggestion. I
must confess that, with all respect for Prezzolini's scholarli-
ness and talent, I do feel a touch of resentment towards him,
because in something he published he said that since there
were absolutely no critics in Italy, only the best writers could
come to the forefront. Thus anonymous wretches were given
another slap in the face. But by this reckoning, Zululand
must offer even more favourable conditions for good writers.

    That unforgettable salon of yours, made gloomy only by
the photograph of Pirandello (to whom I wrote four months
ago sending my novel and a letter without his deigning to

1. Giuseppe Prezzolini, prolific writer and critic, founder editor of *La
Voce* in Florence.

reply, which means I can't stand him, because it isn't enough to write masterpieces; one must also be able to understand *La Coscienza*), that salon has the greatest importance in my life, which I already regard as a *fait accompli*, and I shall never forget it. There is not much chance of my passing through Paris again in the near future because in the firm they think I'm too old to do battle with the Anglo-Saxons. I should be glad of this if it didn't mean that I had lost the chance of coming to thank you personally for what you have wished to do and known how to do for me. You were the only one who never hesitated and did not deign to spend a single word on doubts about the propriety of my language. Now that Prezzolini has read it and not protested, I can sleep easy.

If the *Navire d'Argent* lives up to its name, I shall (perhaps) free myself of my many involvements in underwater paint. In my family (I'm not speaking of my wife), for anyone to believe in literature there must be money in sight. And now I shall also find time to improve my language a little. In the meantime the long, long snake I wrote to you about (entitled *Short Sentimental Journey*) is lying curled up in a drawer. The year's end is threatening and I spend all my days in the office.

How lovely it would be to come and greet you as a real man of letters, to arrive in Paris and find a band at the station! Then to spend a couple of months in that great city, to feel it and know it, far from the great throng of foreigners among whom we usually live! It won't be long, though! While I am writing to you, the sun outside is shining clear and bright. It's cold, but that makes the air more transparent. So I think that instead of my coming to Paris, we need to bring you to Trieste. When will M. Crémieux be free? To move freely and also to write about useful things like *La Coscienza*. My wife joins me in sending greetings and good wishes. If only you knew how often we talk about you, about you all, including the little Crémieux, of whom we caught a glimpse.

Your devoted

Ettore Schmitz.

That winter we went back to London and passed through
Paris again, where we met Mademoiselle Monnier, editor of
the *Navire d'Argent*, the review which was to take over from
Commerce in launching Ettore's work. We were promised
that a whole issue would be given over to Italo Svevo's work.

In fact, while we were in our little house in London one
morning, a French paper arrived around midday. It was
L'Avenir of 27 January 1926. In it was an article signed Leon
Treich, in which the publication of the *Navire d'Argent* was
announced, and Svevo was proclaimed the new star of Italian
literature; he was called 'the Italian Proust'. Ettore was still
in the bathroom. Full of surprise and joy, I called out loudly
to him and he rushed out, wrapped in a towel. Then I saw
him lit up by a vivid, almost ingenuous joy. It was the first
echo his work had made in the world; it was the first review in
an endless series which was to follow in the years to come,
from every continent and in every language.

Having left London, we stopped in Paris to wait for the
publication of the new periodical. Every day found us with
our dear French friends. And then, early in February 1926,
the issue we had been waiting for appeared: it contained a
study by Crémieux of the three novels and some chapters
from *The Confessions of Zeno* and *As a Man Grows Older*.
Ettore returned happily to Trieste with copies of the journal,
impatient to show it to his friends and to spread it around his
circle. This was something he longed to do, a kind of secret
payment for having at last been recognized. He was also
waiting anxiously for the effects of the discovery on the
Italian critics. He was very sensitive to criticism, and ac-
knowledged the justice of negative criticism so much that he
would torture himself because he couldn't do the work again.

When we went through Milan he wanted to take out a
subscription to the *Eco della Stampa*. At the door a group of
young writers surrounded him, led by Eugenio Montale, the
Ligurian poet who had been the first to make an in-depth
study of Svevo, drawing attention to him in Italy, in the

journal *L'Esame* (November–December 1925). They were Lodovici, Somare, Giansiro Ferrata, the son of the painter Tallone, and Leo Ferrero. 'Are you Italo Svevo?' they asked, and cheered him. At first he was speechless, as if stunned: he did not know what to answer. He was so modest that signs of admiration made him shy. Gradually, as his fame grew, he fled more and more from contact with others. I remember that in 1927, setting out on a journey with me, he said: 'Now, no Italo Svevo.'

In Trieste this literary news aroused little interest. Two local critics were pleased – Silvio Benco and Ferdinando Pasini – who alone had grasped the value and inner meaning of Ettore's work when it appeared. A small group of very isolated intellectuals was also interested. But the middlebrow remained indifferent: businessmen continued to see him as a manufacturer who dabbled in literature, rather than as a writer. Ettore was not a popular writer and ingenuously regretted the fact.

Although the doubts inherent in his nature still tormented him, he was swimming in a kind of intoxication. He was overwhelmed by this new life and candidly confessed his satisfaction in it. Among critics and publishers there was now a growing interest in his books. He received letters from strangers. The walls of his inner life opened up to the world. With enthusiasm he discovered what the young were writing in Italy. Now and then he would fall in love with a writer, read everything he had written, talk a great deal about him, and, if possible, correspond with him. For a while it was the age of Pea.[1] D'Annunzio, on the other hand, he could not stand. When we were guests of Signora Marangoni in Florence in 1925, we found a notice above the door of the flat saying [in English] 'Svevo's Club'. There we met Arturo Loria, Elio Vittorini, Raffaello Franchi, Bonsanti and Eugenio Montale. Ettore welcomed and liked them, listened

1. Enrico Pea (1881–1958), a self-taught Italian novelist.

to them enthusiastically, asked about their work, their problems of style, their way of interpreting life. In Trieste he went
to the Caffè Garibaldi where literary men and artists gathered
every evening, people worth knowing like the poet Umberto
Saba, the dialect poet Virgilio Giotti, the writer Giani
Stuparich, the painter Vittorio Bolaffio and the sculptor
Ruggero Rovan; among these the young Bobby Bazlen,[1] who
was one of Ettore's first knowledgeable readers, loved to
linger. In this group Ettore deepened his original interpreta-
tion of the world and of life. Giani Stuparich described these
evenings:

'Lively, amusing and sociable, Italo Svevo could fuse the
company in the Caffè Garibaldi together. Without him, there
were separate groups and some people were silent; with him,
a warmth common to all appeared. With his broad outlook as
a man of the world he opened up the conversation and
clinched this with his own special, kindly smile.

'He talked of London and Florence, but his tone was
always that of Trieste; in him, we all recognized ourselves.
We spoke of poetry and narrative and the figurative arts, and
he never grudged his thoughtful involvement. But he liked
best to talk about people, to anatomize psychological states,
always starting from himself, stripping his own human
nature naked. Profound, talkative, and spontaneous, he was
half-way between an *enfant terrible* who cares nothing for
anyone and a wise old man full of socratic delicacy. Svevo
even managed to make a conquest of Saba.'

However, those most reluctant to recognize his value were
the Italian critics and publishers; and this made him very
surprised and rather sad. When he suggested a second
edition of *Senilità*, Treves replied with a refusal. Impatient
with the delays, Ettore had asked for a definite reply.

1. Roberto Bazlen was a close friend of Svevo's. He introduced
Montale to Svevo's work, and introduced Svevo – and Italy – to Kafka's
work.

I think I have a right to resent the way I have been treated by your firm, [he wrote] . . . Early in March I was kindly received by Signor Dall'Oro, who promised to write to me in a few days about the firm's final decision on whether to publish my novel *Senilità*. As no such letter arrived, I made a second journey to Milan at the end of April. Signor Dall'Oro was very kind and urged me to send a second copy of *Senilità* with the corrections I felt necessary, and promised me a definite reply by 15 May. When I got back to Trieste, I worked intensely, in order to send the copy as soon as possible. I am sixty-five and have no time to lose. A few days later I sent the novel off (and a preface to the second edition), by registered post. So far I have had no reply.

Now, if when you receive this letter a definite decision has not been taken, and the firm of Treves is too much involved with other work and cannot soon go ahead with the reprinting of my novel, then to my great regret I must give up the idea of seeing it published by the firm of Treves. Would you please send the corrected copy, accompanied by the preface, to *L'Esame*, Via Brera 7, asking for a receipt? The corrected copy is of some value to me and I should not like to have to do it again.

You need not write to me, because the staff of *L'Esame* will not fail to let me know that they have received the copy.

As I told Signor Dall'Oro, I can wait no longer and if the firm of Treves is otherwise occupied you have no need to answer this letter.

Yours sincerely
Italo Svevo.

This is the firm's answer, dated 6 July 1926:

'Dear Sir,

'In answer to your request I am returning the copy of *Senilità* and the preface.

'The proposal for the new edition of this book, so warmly recommended by Signor Prezzolini, has come, as you were told, at a time when it is unsuitable for us to take on new projects. The crisis in the firm's administration, caused by the death of our much lamented Signor Beltrami, has, for various reasons, lasted longer than we thought. The new director, now taking over, has been looking at the work in progress and at that which has fallen behind, and has found a backlog which will take up all our time for more than three years; not to mention new works which will inevitably come from writers to whom we are already linked by contracts and former friendly relations. Added to this, production, which for some time has been slowed down by the persistent crisis in the bookshops, cannot be further increased, because the market, which is slow and unmoving, cannot absorb it, and beyond a certain point refuses it. All things considered, while admitting the remarkable quality of a book which deserved far more success than it had, we do not feel that, in the present adverse circumstances, we can try to re-establish it; because if we did so, we should want to do it not for a single volume, but for all your work. I am unhappy not to be able to give you a better answer, and beg you to forgive the delay (due, above all, to our anxious desire to give you a different one).

    'Yours sincerely,
      'O. Dall'Oro.'

Ettore concluded the negotiations with some bitterness:

I received your letter of the 6th, which I understand thus: for three years you are busy and cannot take me on. On the other hand, you would like to publish not just this novel, but all my· work. If you could do that at once, it would be simple; but if one were forced to wait three years it would be impossible. In three years' time, even if I were still alive, I would clearly find it impossible to collaborate in the work, and my collaboration would be necessary. In addition, I am now being talked about, and I am not so presumptuous as to think that some young man in Italy will not overtake me in the same field.

    I have already offered to contribute to the expense of

publishing *Senilità*, the novel which would seem to have aroused most interest in Italy. You refused. And so there is no chance of my gaining the place I hoped for in your firm's list. Thank you for having sent me the corrected copy of *Senilità*.

>Yours sincerely
>Italo Svevo.

To compensate for this disappointment, the French translation of *Zeno*, by Paul-Henri Michel, now appeared. Crémieux had suggested this young writer, who had devoted himself enthusiastically to the translation of Italian works. We had met him in Paris; he welcomed us warmly in his home. While he was doing the translation, Ettore was constantly in touch with him by letter and tried to oppose cuts which Gallimard, editor of the *Nouvelle Revue Française*, wanted to have made.

Your translation satisfied me entirely [he wrote]. Of course I regret the cuts, which I cannot fail to notice, however much I try to follow Signor Crémieux's advice. They are made by an artist, though. One omission I should like restored is Zeno's lack of a sense of rhythm in music. Valery Larbaud spoke to me about it, smiling with pleasure, and it was a smile I loved – the best part of my success. I could not give that up.

I am enclosing with the translation a page on which I suggest some small changes. Please be so kind as to see if you can use them. If you cannot (of seven, five can be judged only by a Frenchman), don't trouble to write to me about them and do what you think best.

Your request seems to me quite sound and comes to me like a present. Your opinion is very important because, after me, you are the one person who knows the novel best. As soon as I received your letter, I wrote to Signor Crémieux, asking him to intervene with the publisher himself. Indeed, I wanted to wait for his reply before writing to you. There would be no point in my writing to Signor Gallimard because that would merely be a third unanswered letter.

I am waiting anxiously to see the next chapter. I hope there
will be no need of more cuts.

The book appeared in France, published by Librairie Gallimard. For the German translation Joyce had advised Ettore to try the firm of Rhein-Verlag, which published all his own work. The translator was a young man from Fiume, Piero Rismondo, who worked in Vienna on the editorial side of the *Wiener Allgemeine Zeitung*. He had turned up as an admirer at our house and offered himself as a translator. It was from the German publisher that Ettore had his first tangible payment for his literary work. He loved making presents so much that he hastened to give me the cheque, in marks, accompanied by a loving note.

Praises and support were unanimous. The only thing Ettore did not accept was the definition of himself as a psychoanalytical writer; so much so that he felt the need to clarify his position on this point. This is the unpublished page where he tried to clarify his thoughts about this:

But there is a science which helps us to study ourselves. Let me say at once what it is: psychoanalysis. Don't be afraid that I shall talk too much about it. I tell you merely to warn you that I have nothing to do with psychoanalysis and I'll give you proof of it. I read some books by Freud in, if I'm not mistaken, 1908. It is now said that *Senilità* and *La Coscienza de Zeno* were written under his influence. As far as *Senilità* is concerned, it is easy for me to reply. I published it in 1899 and psychoanalysis did not exist then; or, in so far as it did exist, it was called Charcot. As for *Coscienza*, for a long time I thought I owed it to Freud, but it appears that I was wrong. Wait: there are two or three ideas in the novel which are actually taken entirely from Freud. The man who, not to attend the funeral of someone he called his friend who was really his enemy, followed the wrong funeral procession, is Freudian, and has a boldness I am proud of. The other man, who dreams of distant events, and in his dreams remoulds them as he would have liked them to be, is Freudian in style, as anyone who knows Freud will realize. It is a paragraph I would be proud of even if it didn't contain another little idea that I'm pleased with. However, for a long time I thought I'd written a work of psychoanalysis. Now I have to say that when I published the book and looked forward to success, as anyone who publishes anything does, there was a deathly silence. Today I can laugh in speaking of it, and I should have been able to laugh at it then if I had been a younger man. Instead, I suffered so much that I invented an axiom: literature is not good for the old. Even a man with my experience of failure could not bear it: it took away my appetite and my sleep. At that time I ran into the only psychoanalytical doctor in Trieste, my good friend Dr Weiss,[1] and, nervously, he looked me in the eye and asked if he was the psychoanalyst in Trieste whom I made fun of in my novel. It was soon clear that it could not be he because during the war years he had not been practising psychoanalysis in Trieste. Reassured, he accepted my book, which I had inscribed for him, promising to study it, and to review it in a psychoanalytical journal in Vienna. For several days I slept and ate better. Success was at hand, because my work was going to be discussed in an internationally-known journal. However, when I saw him again, Dr Weiss told me that he couldn't write about my book because it had nothing whatever to do with psychoanalysis. I was upset by this; for it would have been a great thing if Freud had sent me a telegram saying: 'Thanks for having introduced psychoanalysis into Italian aesthetics.' I would have sent the telegram to Dr Ry of the C.D.S. [*Corriere della Sera*]. Now I am no longer upset. We novelists play games with the great philosophies without really being equipped to expand them. We falsify them, but we also humanize them. The superman, when he arrived in Italy, was not exactly Nietzsche's.

In Italy, he has been brought to life in prose and poetry, and in action too. Whether Nietzsche would recognize him as

1. Edoardo Weiss, from Trieste, a pupil and friend of Freud, and translator of his work into Italian.

his own I don't know, and so much the worse for him if he did
not deny paternity.

But I should like to get the point even more clear, to bring it down to earth even more definitely. I mean, by applying it to a theory much more remote from us than that of the superman; and which has not yet, as far as I know, been even touched by art, but that sooner or later will reach us as a mood or a fantasy.

The theory of relativity cannot for the moment be understood except by those who know how to navigate the waters of higher mathematics. The artist, I mean to say the artist who is either literate or illiterate, after a few vain efforts to approach it, tucks it away in a corner from where it worries and disquiets him, a new basis for scepticism, a mysterious part of the world, without which one can no longer even think. It is there, not forgotten but hidden and cherished beyond biology, and he goes to Einstein and tells him: I have found a way of explaining relativity to ordinary people without making them study mathematics. Encouraged by Einstein, he goes on to describe his idea: suppose a man could be constructed with a heart that, instead of beating seventy-two times a minute, beat only once every ten minutes, clearly this slow man would see the sun pass from one horizon to the other as fast as a rocket. Einstein's response is: It's a good idea, but it has nothing to do with my relativity. Well, anyway, he thought it good, and that's already something. I, who do not understand mathematics or, therefore, genuine relativity, am not sure that there isn't more relativity in the idea than Einstein supposes. It is the artist's destiny to be inspired by a philosopher whom he does not perfectly understand, and the philosopher's destiny not to understand the very artist he inspired. The story of Wagner and Schopenhauer is well known. Wagner sent Schopenhauer his music, protesting his gratitude to the man he considered his master. But Schopenhauer wrote back, saying he thought Rossini's was the music that best suited his philosophy and, as far as he was concerned, it was all he wanted. Today all Schopenhauer's followers are of a different opinion. This intimate relationship between the artist and the philosopher, which is like that of a legal marriage, because like husband and wife they don't really understand each other and yet produce fine children, renews the artist or at least gives him the warmth and feeling of something new, as would happen if it were possible to change part of the dictionary and give us new words purged of the mould and rust of age-long usage. As for the philosopher, he can be called powerful when a powerful reflector sets him in the full glare of the world's stage, he who runs the risk . . .

To hear himself called 'the Italian Proust' astonished Ettore. He did not read Proust until 1926. It was Signora Crémieux who asked him, on our first visit to Paris: 'Do you know Proust? No? And yet you resemble each other.' Ettore immediately asked about the French writer, bought all his books and set out to read them with great interest. He left a judgement on Proust in an unpublished piece sketching parallels between him and Joyce:

I am not a critic and as I read over these notes I doubt whether I have given you a clear idea of this novel. I am still trying to make it clear. It seems to me important to establish that there is no analogy between his work and Proust's. Joyce, in Italy, is always mentioned alongside Proust. I should like definitely to separate them. It is quite an easy task. They met only once. One night Proust, who was already very ill, decided to leave his home with the sealed-up windows on the Champs-Élysées, probably because he needed to make an inquiry and so be able to end some sentence he was writing, or some image he was fixing about a real event. He was introduced to Joyce and, distracted from his own preoccupation, asked him out of the blue: 'Do you know Princess X?' 'No,' said Joyce. 'Nor do I want to in the very least.' They parted and never met again.

I think that if the two great writers were to meet, each on his own ground, and in the sphere of his own art, and one of them were to shout (being so far from the other) 'Brother, do

you recognize this?' the other would reply: 'No, nor do I
want to in the very least.'

Proust is the artist of the great prose narrative. His sentences are creative through the force of their own completeness; they evolve as they go ahead, and each one is a discovery, a surprise. It is not enough for him to narrate; he is urged to narrate by the nostalgic need to seek the time which is no longer there. On his canvas feature is added to feature, colour to colour, in order to adhere to reality. The painting's perfect tonality results from a perfect vision of reality. His narrative seems to lack a plan. What need is there for one, seeing that the events which have taken place cannot lack order?

And when this reality of his becomes satire, it becomes so almost without his intervention. Reality can sometimes make itself heard solely through precision.

But Joyce is entirely the opposite. He is the artist who has prepared the whole plan of adventure from which the characters will arise. He takes what he likes best from reality and out of it makes something so complete that it takes the place of reality. I don't think he even knows how to work on a canvas. He must mould his figures before painting them and fill his workplace with three-dimensional creatures who are so much alive that it is as if they speak and move without anyone's help. The austere writer makes us forget that he could help them. We see him as unmoved because he hides his own effort.

In Proust, reality becomes a science. Each of his characters is studied in his or her origins and organs.

In Joyce there is no sign of such a study. Others (the reader) may make it, since the complete person has been handed over to them. I have tried to dissect him myself, and God knows what I have made of him. But one's joy in Joyce's work does not spring from such analysis (not even from mine). The obscurity which hangs over his book is the product of all sorts of unstated aims, and through his unexpected intellectual fate it slowly clears; the reader then finds he has collaborated with an incomparable guide in the creation of the whole world, a known one, yet as mysterious as the one from which it was copied. This accounts for the cries of surprise and admiration from so many outstanding critics. I understand very well what the great poet and critic T.S. Eliot means when he says that anyone who imitates . . . [incomplete].

Ettore commented to Benjamin Crémieux on his panoramic study of Italian literature:[1]

Trieste, Villa Veneziani, 5 May 1928

Dear Friend,

On the 2nd of this month your book arrived and I have already devoured it. The whole work, in its incisiveness and brevity, is a jewel, a precious gift for which each one of us should be grateful. I don't mean those of us you mention, but Italians in general. As for me, like a true vain old man, nothing is ever enough; and yet you have spoiled me. It is true that presenting me in a *Panorama* is like putting a clove of garlic in the kitchen of people who don't like the smell. But as an Italian and your friend I am proud of your work, which is both tactful and perfectly independent. In your hands this half century has acquired a great importance. A work of such objectivity could only come from abroad, but it could also be written only by a foreigner who is as little a foreigner as you are. When I try to remember how you walked through our streets when you were staying among us, I cannot help thinking you found a way of moving along a superstructure, a higher level, which allowed you to see better, but above all meant that you were not involved in the scuffles down below. The biographies of Carducci, Pascoli and Panzini[2] are delightful. Admirable too, and so much more difficult from the scientific point of view, is that of Croce. I love the way you show the Italian state of mind at the outbreak of war: obviously true, and yet surprising even to us who lived through it. There is something epic about the struggle of

1. *Panorama de la littérature italienne contemporaine* (1928).
2. Eminent Italian authors of the late nineteenth and early twentieth centuries.

small people against circumstances and history. You describe 103
it with affection which can be derived only from a perfect
knowledge of men and affairs.

I am sure that your work can arouse nothing but gratitude
in Italy. If my expression of it is not the first, that's because of
the slowness of our bookshops. When one puts down the
book, one has a feeling of having heard the noblest part of our
history over the past fifty years.

And now I'm more than ever certain that you'll never
abandon Italy. Every day I gaze at the horizon: are the
Crémieux coming, or not? They must pass this way on their
way to Romania! If I hear you've been through Trieste
without calling me to see you, I shall never look you in the
face again . . .

On 16 May he took up the subject of the book again with
Crémieux. This extract shows how he did not hesitate to ask
for the writers of Trieste to be treated fairly.

. . . here we are in Venezia Giulia and there's no mention of
Attilio Hortis and Silvio Benco in your book. As far as Benco
is concerned, I'm really sorry. He is an artist eaten up almost
entirely by journalism and a little by D'Annunzio. You may
say that if he's eaten up, then he's no longer seen. But your
book is full of people who have been eaten up. Benco (and, to
come closer to you, I'll forget his first two novels for the
moment, which deep down are far less D'Annunzian than
they seem) is, if nothing else, a great cultural popularizer.

After the appearance of the French translation of Ettore's
work, something happened in Italy as well. Italian critics had
been arguing with the French, almost complaining of the
halo of glory which they had given an Italian writer. It was
then that the publisher Morreale made concrete proposals,
and in 1927 the second edition of *As a Man Grows Older*
appeared, which Ettore had completely revised stylistically.
In the preface he testified to his gratitude to James Joyce,
who had been able, as he put it, to:

renew the miracle of Lazarus: . . . That a writer whose own work weighed upon him so urgently should spend valuable time on helping his less fortunate brethren is so generous that, I think, it explains his own astounding success, because every other word of his, all the words which make up his enormous work, are expressed by the same great soul.

But he also wanted to give Joyce a present, something very dear to his heart which he valued a great deal: the portrait Veruda had painted of me when I was young.

Trieste, 27 March 1928

Dear Friend,

I have found here the two letters to publishers. No one could be more generous than that.

I am living on the sounds which accompany me from Paris. One is heard more loudly than the rest: Anna Livia and the portrait by Veruda. Would you like it? Put the word 'Yes' on a postcard and I'll send it. Without your agreement I daren't not send you the portrait of my wife. I have many works by Veruda; as for the subject, I hold the original very dear.

He was burning with impatience, in a tremendous hurry to see all his books reprinted. In an article in *Solaria*, which appeared after his death, the French translator Paul-Henri Michel wrote:

'During the year 1926, while I was translating *La Coscienza di Zeno*, Italo Svevo followed the stages of my work with an anxiety that all his letters reveal. He was afraid of dying before this translation, to which he was kind enough to attribute great importance, was completed. If things did not go as fast as he would have liked, his letters became quite despairing. It was at about this time that I received the manuscript of "Una Burla Riuscita",[1] dated 14 October

1. 'The Hoax', a story in which an author is tricked into believing that a big foreign publisher wishes to buy the rights to a novel he wrote forty years previously.

Increasingly, the anxiety grew in him that he would not
live to see all the possibilities his fame allowed him to hope for
realized. 'I therefore wrote and told him,' Paul-Henri Michel
went on, 'that Gallimard were not like his Westermann,
something imaginary; whereupon Italo Svevo replied that he
wasn't much reassured, adding the words: "I really feel I've
become Mario Samigli".'[1]

The obscure presentiment of his imminent death weighed
upon him. The very joy of success was shadowed by clouds.
To his dear friend Madame Crémieux he wrote:

16 March 1926

Dear Signora and Dear Friend,

The man who writes to you now is almost famous. Every
paper in Italy – some more, some less – has mentioned me in
terms which are more or less flattering. There's no question
of criticism. They say it will come. Meantime they throw
Rigutini and Fornaciari[2] at my head, heavy stuff, but it
doesn't hurt me. I am always surprised at the effect of
Crémieux's powerful kick. I am known to everyone. Even in
Trieste they begin to be pleased to have me among them . . .
for a short while longer.

If I told you I was better before, I'd be lying, because I
remember my surly impatience, which made me snarl at my
neighbours. I can tell you, though, that I imagined I'd be
better than in fact I am. You can see, from me, that no one is
ever quite well in this world. They say that's what brings
progress.

And I want progress! May I have two words, just two
words, from the person who comforted me at the time of my

1. Westermann is the big Viennese publisher and Mario Samigli the
author in Svevo's story 'The Hoax' (see previous note).
2. Giuseppe Rigutini and Raffaello Fornacieri, orthodox writers on
classical Italian literature.

childish impatience? Why must I be without them, now that I'm so much better? I trust your dear family, that is you, your husband and little Francis, are well. God knows whether your husband has received my book with the cuts of 10 pages, 2 lines and ½ a word? Would you work on the translation? If so, lose no time in sending me an empty postcard, without even a signature. It will truly be a great joy to me.

I kiss your hand.

Yours devotedly

Ettore Schmitz.

'Paris, 6 April 1926

'Dear Great Friend,

'What can you be thinking of my silence? I delayed so long because I was always hoping to be able to tell you that I would retain the honour of translating you; but alas my incessant migraines, and the very natural impatience for this translation that I can sense on your part, make it necessary, as a matter of loyalty, to renounce it. I regret it intensely, as you will easily believe, and I envy the lucky man without migraine who will undertake this interesting task. You can be sure that it will be reviewed here and that the glory of Svevo will not suffer because of my withdrawal. Yes, you are a famous man, and at last your compatriots are doing you justice and are more and more giving you recognition. Everything arrives in the end. When are you coming to Paris again? I hope it will be soon, and at a moment when I have not fled the nest. All the Italians with whom we have discussed you are enchanted with *La Coscienza di Zeno*, and in particular Buontempelli [sic!][1] who was in Paris recently and told us he was preparing a long essay on you. I hope that piece of news gives you more pleasure than my withdrawal gives you pain. For after all, one can always replace a translator, but a good critic, and above all an Italian one, is not so easily replaced.'

1. Massimo Bontempelli, prominent Italian poet, playwright, critic and teacher.

Meanwhile, Benjamin Crémieux kept him informed and reassured about the way the translation of *The Confessions of Zeno*, which P.-H. Michel was working on, was progressing. But Madame Crémieux had become silent again, and Ettore wrote to her, asking for news.

15 January 1927

Dear, Much Valued Signora,

For a long time we have had no news of you. I didn't write before because it seemed that I should have to go to London, a tiresome journey which would have had as its prize a day or two's stay in Paris. Now it's certain that I shan't move, and so I'd love to have your news. Your little family has been pretty overwhelmed recently. Quite unjustly, since you are so young and so good. I hope to have a line from you, and set you a good example giving you news of myself: I live very quietly, calmly waiting for the French translation of my novel. What contributes to my serenity is the large amount of work in my office since the end of the year.

Have you read my story which was refused by the Princess of Versailles? Here in Italy I have had some satisfaction, but tiny, very small. Binazzi[1] of Bologna sent me a few lines saying I had given Italy a work of art. They are still against me, and, to tell the truth, I am now glad they are.

So write, dear lady; greetings and sincere good wishes from my wife,

I remain your ever devoted and grateful friend
Ettore Schmitz.

Madame Crémieux replied affectionately:

'Wednesday, 2 February 1927

'My Very Dear Great Friend,

'I am very behindhand with you, and you have had the kindness to interest yourself in my poor destiny. For two months I have really been very ill. I am getting better at last;

1. Bino Binazzi, literary critic who wrote for an influential Bologna newspaper.

and one of the first smiles of this week of convalescence has come from *Zeno*, who is now expressed in limpid French after having charmed me in an Italian which only pedants found without grace. Do you know that the translation is almost finished? (It is remarkable, and will be finished in a fortnight at most; my husband and I will be going through it this evening, reading it side by side and marvelling for a second time at what the book contains.) I am now quite sure that you will receive the glory due to you and that your *Zeno* will have an enormous success.

'My husband is going to write to you himself, but he asked me to tell you now that he hopes your book will appear in May or June. It will thus be associated with the sweetness of holidays and will come to life in charming hands by the seaside or at the foot of mountains. Had you thought of that? You must certainly come to Paris to see that it is well displayed in booksellers' windows. Do not sadden yourself by saying that you will never be here again; you now have not only friends (and I claim to be in the front rank of them, how presumptuous!), but a precious child, a child who has lost none of his novelty and charm through transplantation but who is, none the less, in a country not his own and is in need, from time to time, of the warmth of your presence. We have received the *novella*; I have read it with great interest, but my husband has not yet done so, nor Larbaud. But he will write to you soon. Au revoir, dear friend; best wishes for the year to you and to yours and to *Zeno* also.

'Your faithful

'M. Crémieux.'

While he was still waiting anxiously for the appearance of his novel in France, he replied to Benjamin Crémieux:

Trieste, 15 March 1927

Dearest Friend,

I received your kind letter of the 12th. If it does nothing else, my story about poor Samigli can show you how I was waiting for the translation of my book. Certainly it will be a great joy, minimized by the *coupures*. My gratitude to you is not minimized by any such *coupures*.

Obviously the stories will not do. I see from your letter that 'Generous Wine' will not do for the *Commerce* either. I think it is clear that the old man had better rest on his laurels. I had a nice letter from M. Michel, to which I answered at once, giving him leave to translate 'The Hoax' at my expense. This is really the last thing I did. I thought of it when that woman journalist from Trieste invaded your home and wrote to Trieste. Then nothing came for a long time (until I landed up in Paris) and in the meantime I consoled myself by writing. I wrote and re-wrote and it is what it is; I could not improve it. Whereas 'Generous Wine' is very old. I think even Joyce read it in 1914. I learnt that *Commerce* could not use 'The Hoax' and revised 'Generous Wine'. But in rather a hurry. So I shouldn't like to translate it again. I'll think about it, bearing in mind your two remarks. If I don't know what else to do, it will be there. In the last number of *Commerce* I found some essays by someone called Barilli. They interested me very much. It seems that we shall meet among the Italian writers in Paris. Recently I have found two worthwhile Italian writers: Giani Stuparich, from Trieste, a friend of Slataper, who published *Colloquio con mio fratello*, a book that is like a temple. Last week I happened to have *Moscardino* by Pea (published by Treves) in my hands, a really strange and wonderful book, in a rough Tuscan like that of Tozzi.[1] Some pages have a strength and clarity which make one envious. I expect you know both: Vociani.[2] All the little good we have went that way. If 'The Hoax' (to get back to myself) cannot be placed, I shall keep the translation as a beloved memento.

In Milan, where I went last week, I lectured to the *Convegno* on James Joyce. My wife says I did it well. The audience were all women, Ferrieri[3] made me read at 5 in the

1. Federigo Tozzi, novelist, poet and playwright.
2. i.e. writers for the Florentine periodical *La Voce*.
3. Enzo Ferrieri was the editor of *Il Convegno*.

afternoon when the men were at work. That's what Sacchi told me. The *Corriere della Sera*, which is always so nice to me, didn't mention it. I have heard from friends that every time Caprin[1] speaks of me he raises his voice. The *Secolo* had a short very friendly article. Today I sent the manuscript to Joyce and shan't think of it again. I also think I shan't lecture in public again.

Thanks and greetings from my wife and all the family to your wife and yourself. We were very glad to hear the signora is completely recovered. When shall we meet again?

Believe me, dearest friend, your affectionate
Ettore Schmitz.

The next number of *Convegno* will publish my story about that lady-killer who was looking for his mother and found her.[2] Do you remember?

The long-awaited time when *The Confessions of Zeno* would appear in Paris was approaching. Benjamin Crémieux asked Ettore for a biographical note and a photograph, for its publication.

This was his reply:

[September-October 1927]

Dearest Friend,

I am truly touched by the kindness you show me, by the generous tone of your letter, which becomes more moving through your words of regret for poor Cantoni.[3] I shall keep the letter as a precious gift. It is anything but a gesture of politeness. But are you coming through Trieste? I should so much love the chance to shake your hand. Don't forget me if you come this way. If you come only to Venezia Giulia I should be able to give you a Sunday and meet you then.

Here, in a few lines, is my biography: Born in 1861 in

---

1. Giulio Caprin, a *Corriere della Sera* critic hostile to Svevo.

2. 'The Mother', a fable in which a cockerel sets out to find his mother, and does so, to ill-effect.

3. The writer Ettore Cantoni had died in Milan the previous August (1927).

Trieste. My grandfather was a German state employee at
Treviso; my grandmother and mother were Italian. At the
age of 12 I was sent to Germany to a commercial school,
where I studied rather less than I might have done. However,
I became passionately interested in German literature in
those years. At 17 I went to the higher commercial school, the
'Revoltella' in Trieste, where I rediscovered my Italianness.
At 19 into a bank; in *Una Vita* the part about the bank and the
public library is truly autobiographical.

At 36 I had the good fortune to join an industrial firm,
where I am still working. Until the war broke out I was very
busy, mainly directing the workers in Trieste, Murano
(Venice) and London. At 30 I published *Una Vita* and at 37
Senilità. Then I decided to give up literature, which
obviously diminished my business capacity, and I dedicated
my few free hours to the violin, so as to stop nursing literary
dreams. The war removed me from business, and the long
rest was the reason why, in 1919, I started to write *La
Coscienza*, which was published in 1923.

That is all. A life that may not seem very full but was
adorned with so many happy affections that I would gladly
live it over again.

I'm afraid I have given you more than you ask for. But this
is a fault which can easily be corrected.

Here is my photograph. It was taken in 1926. I put off
sending it because my wife is in the country and – thank
heaven – I have none of the keys.

Thank you once again.

A warm handshake, Yours ever

    Ettore Schmitz.

Ettore much enjoyed meeting the young. To Alberto
Rossi[1] he wrote:

You guessed; my success among our readers is certainly not
great. But (as you said yourself) from the crowd I don't

---

1. A critic who had just published an article entitled 'Svevo e Charlot
[i.e. Charlie Chaplin]' in the Turin *Gazzetta del Popolo*, 5 July 1928.

belong to, a friend sometimes emerges who holds out a hand. So in Italy I am a man with many successes. So many young people, one at a time, greet me as if I were one of them and I enjoy this more than if I had a single big success.

Yet he suffered from not being a popular writer. 'A bookshop assistant said to me: "You are an author who doesn't go." And so it is,' he told me one day with some bitterness. To Ferrero he wrote: 'I should so much like to be here for the success of *Senilità*. I know that Morreale's[1] rep., a practical man who used to travel for Cappelli, said when he saw my name: "There's an author who doesn't go".' This was his secret sorrow and he enjoyed imagining success of an American kind:

I know, because nothing surprising has ever happened to me in my whole life and, to put it crudely, I've never had a stroke of luck. All these things were *going* to happen to me and I imagined them, but with rather too much energy. An American comes to buy my novel for 100,000 dollars. I see him with his smooth face and gold teeth. He's come to talk business. 'How much?' he asks. I am modest in my demands: 'A hundred thousand dollars on condition I have the translator of my choice, for I don't want my novel to be badly written, even in English; also, in view of my age, an agreement that it is to be published as soon as possible.' The American agrees. We go to the lawyer to sign the contract and I see the document which resembles the one I signed before; except that, beside the block capitals saying: *Oggetto immobile . . .*, there's written: *Il mobile*[2] *. . . : La Coscienza di Zeno.* Hesitantly the lawyer asks: 'Is a hundred thousand agreed? We must decide, because if not there will be more stamp duty.' 'I'm happy with a hundred thousand.' If I raised it by as much as a single dollar the American's smooth face might

1. Giuseppe Morreale, the Milan publisher of the second edition of *As a Man Grows Older*.
2. i.e. 'House' and 'Furnishings': the pun is untranslatable.

darken and he might resign himself to buying a novel
recommended by the *Corriere della Sera*. Then it's signed and
I go out with my cheque for a hundred thousand dollars.

Of course, something imagined with such precision has no
need actually to take place.

At home he never talked about writers and publishers; he
mentioned his work briefly and occasionally read me a few
pages.

Letizia could not be much involved in her father's work;
her husband's strong personality dominated her entirely, and
she was busy looking after the children. Although we all lived
together, and felt tenderly towards one another, she never
imagined her father's inner turmoil, which he was careful to
keep secret.

Ettore visited the young men of the *Quindicinale*,[1] edited
by Somarè, which in December 1925 and January 1926 had
published Eugenio Montale's revealing articles. One evening, as he came out of the office surrounded by them, he said
to Lodovici: 'I come out of the *Quindicinale* feeling I've been
through an *Esame*.'[2] He loved making jokes like this, and
sometimes made several in a row, as if his greatest pleasure
lay in making his friends laugh. Even with me, he always
tried to be amusing, especially when we were travelling. I
don't think I ever laughed as much as I did on our journeys:
he was always in a joking mood. One day, in London, he
went to a photographer, and asked him, seriously and
demurely, to take a fine photograph. 'I am a professional
dancer,' he said, 'and I need a fine photo.' The photographer
looked dubiously at the old gentleman, staring uncertainly at
his rather stout figure and bald head. One morning I was
visiting the Louvre in my usual methodical and conscientious
way when Ettore, who quickly tired of admiring statues and

1. Literary periodical in Milan where *L'Esame* (also edited by Enrico
Somarè) was based.
2. 'Esame' is the Italian word for exam or examination.

paintings, said: 'If you don't get me out of here soon, I'll pull the Venus de Milo down on your head.' His own head was very large and we could never find a hat to fit him; we enjoyed wandering round the shops, looking for that hat which never could be found.

More than the sights of nature, more than art, he loved the sight of people, for whom he had a special sense. 'To scold someone who has no right to answer back means falsifying one's own relationship with him entirely,' he wrote. 'He'll never be sincere with you again. He'll be set below you, that's fine, but inside himself he'll hate and despise you.' He also observed animals very closely, especially dogs and birds. His observation of dogs is reflected in 'Argo and His Master'. The sparrows which flew round the house were also a source of interest and enjoyment. Every day he prepared breadcrumbs for them, and stood peering out of the window, watching their ceaseless movement. Children he adored. His first great friend had been his nephew Umbertino, son of his sister Ortensia, who was left an orphan at fourteen months when his mother died. Then Letizia's children were born, Piero, Paolo and Sergio. Sergio was the most like him, in the shape of his head, in his thoughtful expression, and in his love of intellectual problems. Ettore loved going for long walks with the children, during which he held mysterious conversations, traces of which remain in his writings. Yet, despite all this serenity and joy, his eyes, which so often glittered cheerfully, teasingly, betrayed a dark degree of suffering which I was unable to understand; while sometimes they were full of a strange surprise: 'Well, what am I? Not someone who lives, but someone who describes.'

THE 'CONVEGNO' OPENED its doors to him at once. On our frequent visits to Milan (we now always travelled together) we used to go to its fine rooms, and to Signora Ferrieri's hospitable drawing-room. It was at the *Convegno* that Ettore gave his first lecture. On 26 March 1927 he spoke about Joyce, dealing particularly with *Ulysses*. Although he was unused to an audience, he was quite unruffled that evening, reading his many note-cards in a clear calm voice, which even when he spoke Italian kept its Triestine accent.

In Paris, a superb public occasion took place during a meeting of the PEN Club, in which fifty literary people took part. Benjamin Crémieux was the organizer of literary dinners of this kind in honour of eminent European writers passing through Paris. The dinner in Italo Svevo's honour was to celebrate the publication of *The Confessions of Zeno* in French. Also honoured at the dinner were the Russian Isaak Babel, author of *Red Cavalry*, and the Romanian poet Ion Pillat.

The white horseshoe-shaped table ran along the walls. Ettore sat in the middle, beside Crémieux and Jules Romains, who introduced the writers being honoured and spoke about them. I was sitting beside Joyce, who after dinner confided in Giovanni Comisso, the only other Italian writer present at the banquet: 'They say I've immortalized Svevo, but I've also immortalized Signora Svevo's hair. She had long blonde hair. My sister has seen it loose and told me about it. Near Dublin there's a river which passes a dyer's shop and its water is as reddish as that table; so I've enjoyed talking about those two things which resemble each other in the book I'm writing. A woman in it will have this hair, which is Signora Svevo's.' He was alluding to the little book, *Anna Livia Plurabelle*, for which he had also taken my name, afterwards writing jokingly to my husband: 'Talking of names, I've just given your wife's name to the main character of the book I'm writing. Ask her, however, not to take up arms, either of steel or fire, since the person involved is the

Pyrrha of Ireland (or rather of Dublin) beside which (her name is Anna Liffey) the seventh city of Christendom springs up. All I took from her was her hair, and that only on loan, to adorn the little river of my city, the Anna Liffey, which would be the longest river in the world if it were not the canal which comes from afar to join the great god Anthony the Worker of Miracles, and then, having changed its mind, returns whence it came.'

Beside Joyce sat his wife, who was delighted to talk in Triestian dialect with me again, and then Ivan Goll, Jean Paulhan, MacOrlan, Ilya Ehrenburg, Martin Maurice and many others. Ettore regretted that he was unable to return Romains' courteous words by talking to him about his books, because he had not read them; but next day he made haste to buy them, and he read them as soon as he returned to Trieste.

He had a vehement, unspoiled curiosity to know every-thing. He read a great deal, especially at night, and often woke me to read aloud some passage which had struck him. His last literary love was Kafka, about whom he kept meaning to write an essay or a description. Young critics and literary men who were passing through and wanted to meet him often turned up at our house. It was Italo Svevo they came to see, no longer Mr Schmitz, and they also now came to the parties in the Villa Veneziani. Ettore welcomed them delightedly and loved showing them the hidden beauties of Trieste. He would take them by car along the marina of Barcola as far as the white castle of Miramare, and make them climb the steep, narrow, colourful streets of the Old City in whose houses the real people of Trieste swarmed; then on to the old castle of San Giusto, to see the magnificent bay, and Trieste itself which, in his words, 'with its white houses along the shore embraces the sea in a big semicircle, and looks as if its shape had been given it by a huge wave which pushed it back towards the centre of the city'. He took them to the Garden of Monuments, pausing before the one to Winckel-mann. Once he took Pirandello and Marta Abba to the caves

of Postumia.[1] To his favourite guests he loved talking about
books, races and nations, subjects he particularly loved.
Without losing any of his simplicity he touched on the
subtlest, the most hidden feelings of the human heart, and in
his talk even the simplest anecdote revealed an unknown
world. When Leo Ferrero came to our house, he said, as he
introduced him: 'You see, she hasn't got a squint,' referring
to the character of Augusta, Zeno's wife, who was completely
different from me physically, but in whom he had painted my
moral portrait.

Eugenio Montale, Giacomo Debenedetti, Umberto Saba
and many others, including foreigners, also came to our
house. Their talk touched on all human problems. Ettore
took no interest in politics, except as a curious observer, with
perhaps a touch of scepticism.

The Lord God became a socialist [he wrote in a fable]. He
abolished hell and purgatory, and set everyone in an equal
place in Heaven, where they were in eternal happiness. A
certain rich man then died and was amazed to find himself
welcomed in paradise, but he soon got used to his new
existence and even began to complain of it. 'What's the
matter with you?' asked God, in a huff. 'Oh Lord, send me
back to Earth! This isn't really heaven, here, you don't see
anyone suffering!'

But humble people approached Ettore too, and unknown
people came to tell him about their problems. He listened to
them all with humanity, for he knew how to listen. He also
gave good advice. But this happened before he was famous.
His great goodness and benevolence were well known in the
city; he forgave everything, and always found extenuating
circumstances, even for those who had done him wrong.

Although he was well aware of its value, success did not
turn his head at all. One day I asked him: 'Ettore, did you

1. Marta Abba was an Italian actress who worked closely with
Pirandello and subsequently translated many of his plays into English.

always know you were worth something?' and he answered me with profound conviction: 'Yes, I always thought I'd done something good.'

He had started working again, although he doubted whether he had the strength for it. 'What can a man of nearly seventy do?' he asked. Talking to friends he said: 'The time of illusions has passed. Mine is just a golden sunset.' To me he often said regretfully: 'I shall have to leave you soon,' and so insistently that I was shocked and begged him not to say it again. He was no longer the man he had once been, merry and full of witticisms; after the first intoxication something in him had weakened, as if the great flame of success had consumed his vitality. His sound sleep became restless. He had always avoided consulting doctors, and did not do so now, nor did he take medicines; he had never managed to stay in bed for longer than forty-eight hours; yet he thought constantly about illness and death, listening to his body with intense attention. Sometimes he raised his right arm with his fist clenched, as if to ward off an invisible enemy, and said, in a breathless voice: 'I can hear him coming, I can hear him coming.' And if I asked him 'What can you hear?' he would answer, 'The blow.' (This is the word ['il colpo'] used in our dialect to mean a stroke.) But for many years he had been obsessed with the idea of physical decay. A note of his, dated 10 October 1899, says:

It is strange that the fact of birth implies the pain of death, and even stranger that I, at nearly forty, am surprised by this. It proves that there is something of boyish ingenuousness in me still and I am glad of it. Yesterday evening I was on the point of sleep when this macabre idea struck me. I wondered anxiously if this bent towards pain and death had already begun in me. I got as far as imagining a dark, burning, continuous, irremediable pain, without relief or pause. I realized that the capacity to breathe a little air is something which cannot be purchased with all the goods at our disposal. Then I began to imagine the death of an eye . . .

He tried to live in a way that would give him a regular, healthy life. He loved the car, but preferred long walks on the outskirts of Trieste and often walked the fairly long distance between our house at Servola and the Stock Exchange. In the last years, having put on weight, for he had always had a good appetite and liked solid meals, he had given up having supper, and instead took a glass of milk and some fruit; after which he would go up to the apartment of my brother-in-law Oberti, who had a splendid collection of records, and for a couple of hours would enjoy listening to classical music. The only rule of health which he had not managed to obey was the one which forbade smoking. Giving up his thirty or forty cigarettes a day would have been the one thing which would have done him good. His lungs were already very worn and the threat of lung cancer hung over him. And yet he loved life. In all its manifestations he felt it as powerful and beautiful, in great things and small. And, despite having studied their least noble instincts profoundly, he loved people and knew that unsuspected depths are hidden even in ordinary things.

In this, his physical decline, he was dominated by the wish to write. In 1926 he wrote some short stories: 'The Mother', of which I remember a first draft made in 1910, a kind of fable so good that, in a lecture given by Professor Ferdinando Pasini at the University of Trieste soon after Ettore's death, it was read to the audience with the comment that it would be worthy of any anthology. It was in fact translated into many languages. Then he wrote 'The Hoax', which reflected the narrow life of Trieste in wartime, 'Generous Wine', in which the real protagonist is illness, and 'The Story of the Nice Old Man and the Pretty Girl' in which he faced the final age of man, describing the state of physical decay in someone ageing, and condensing the great mass of observations he had made on the threshold of old age which had opened up unexplored horizons for him. Then he set to work ardently on a book which was to be the crown of his career, but which was cut short by his death. He took up the character of Zeno, but a Zeno who had aged. It was still the same theme, developed further on in time: in April 1927 he had confided to a critic: 'Perhaps people will realize that I have written only one novel in my whole life; all the more should I not be forgiven if it were badly written.' The rough sketches left make it clear that this book was begun in the spring of 1928. One sheet begins thus:

On 2 January 1927, Signor Giovanni Respiro wrote in a book he had bought to write his memoirs in: 'Le Confessioni di un Vegliardo' ('The Confessions of an Old Man'). [As the work went ahead Signor Giovanni had become Zeno again, an aged Zeno.] I shall therefore describe the present and that part of the past which has still not disappeared, not to preserve the memory of it but to collect my thoughts. [4th April 1928.] How much alive this life is, and how definitely dead is the part I didn't tell; I go looking for it, sometimes anxiously, feeling incomplete, but it cannot be found again. And I also know that the part I've told about isn't the most important. It became important because I scrutinized it, but now what am I? Not the man who lived, but the man who described. Oh, the only part of life is collecting one's thoughts! When everyone understands that as clearly as I do, then everyone will write; life will be literaturized. Half humanity will dedicate itself to reading and studying what the other half has noted, and contemplation will occupy more time than anything else and so will be subtracted from real, horrible life. And if one part of human kind rebels and refuses to read the other half's effusions, so much the better. Everyone will read himself instead; and people's lives will have a chance to repeat, to correct, to crystallize themselves, whether or not they become clearer in the process. For good or evil, they won't go on being as they are now, flat and insignificant, buried as soon as born, with all their days melting into each other, piling up indistinguishably into years and decades.

By now he worked with a certain difficulty. Perhaps his

heart was tired, though his intellect was still lively, and indeed even richer. The fame he had achieved imposed a greater responsibility upon him, and the problem of language tormented him more than ever. In our house at Opicina, called the Villa Letizia, which he loved, where he spent his last summer, he must have rewritten many pages of his new work. The house stood at the edge of the town, towards the road to Banne, surrounded by old pine trees and horse-chestnuts. In summer it was a cool, delightful refuge.

Letizia had collected seventeenth-century furniture – Italian peasant pieces in the dining-room, copper engravings on the walls, and a number of wooden plaques, carved in relief, which had been used to press designs on to fabrics, and as butter moulds. There was even an antique spinet. Our room was on the first floor. We had our meals with Letizia and the children. Ettore often took walks towards the scented pine woods and the Obelisk, where he could take in the whole of Trieste: a sea of houses between the mountains and the bay, the blue carpet of the waves, the coast of Istria just sketched on the horizon. In twenty minutes the car would take us down the picturesque slopes to the city. Ettore went down every day to go to the office.

In April 1927 he had the joy of hearing that Anton Giulio Bragaglia had staged a short dramatic work of his, called *Terzetto Spezzato* (*The Broken Trio*), in Rome. The critics called it curious, original, interesting, but not much was heard of it by the public. The theatre, which was Ettore's secret love, never gave him the satisfaction he hoped for. It had been the first of his artistic dreams, and remained something he longed for, which had always attracted him passionately. Throughout his life he was one of the most assiduous theatre-goers at seasons of the Teatro Verdi, and on our travels abroad we never failed to go to the most significant performances of plays in London and Paris. 'The form of forms, the theatre, the only one where life can transmit itself directly and precisely,' he used to call it.

Until his last years he revised and re-revised the manuscripts of his plays. But there was always something in the
development of the action that worried him. He had worked
hard to bring the complexity of his ideas to the stage and was
always doubtful of the success of his efforts. He had often
discussed with Silvio Benco the third act of his play *A
Husband*, his best work for the theatre. The complexity of the
questions it raised made it the most important of his plays; so
did its outstanding secondary characters, which he nonetheless tried to change. Then he had done nothing about it. He
had turned for advice to a famous dramatist whom I suppose
to be Pirandello – and he had not replied. Among his
manuscript papers I found the draft of a letter:

Dear Sir,

An unknown man is writing to you. Years ago I published
a novel which was praised by Domenico Oliva and others. It
seems that my critics had little influence on the public,
because my novel had little success. I remain in my corner,
but I can assure you that I have followed the careers of my
more fortunate colleagues with complete sympathy and no
rancour of any sort. This does honour to my character but
also (and I mention it only because I want to find a word
which will make you trust me, as I need) to my critical
discernment. In fact, to succeed, it is not enough to offer
good and perhaps original ideas; one must present oneself
whole, fashioned, finished. Whereas I am an unlucky fellow
who knows how to do all sorts of things half-heartedly, but
nothing completely. I never understood this deficiency of
mine so well as when I came to write a play. You know how
the fabric of a play has to be lucid and clear, however complex
the thought that sustains it may be. I know this too, but the
wretched thing is that when I seek after this lucidity (and
seeking it is quite wrong), everything withers in my poor
hands, which cut, add, and deform everything and cannot
cast that ray of light on my work which may split in the prism
but in such a way that it cannot be re-formed. Is it a matter of

the ear or of the hand? I don't know, and unless you help me I
probably never shall.

I do not presume to criticize your plays but what is certain is that among your gifts there gleams brightly the quality which I lack: among our writers I looked for the one who would be most shocked by deficiency and found it was you.

Now, I am not yet asking you to rewrite my play; I shall dare only to propose it to you when you have accepted it and when you have been so kind as to agree to the proposal which at the moment . . . I have not made to you.

I am, dear sir, yours sincerely
Italo Svevo.

The fact is that Pirandello did not understand him and this lack of understanding was one of the final bitter things in Ettore's life. With the established stars of Italian letters he had no luck. He had never tried to approach D'Annunzio, for whom he really had no liking, and who had, in his turn, ignored Ettore.

It was the young writers, gifted with a new sensitivity, who sought him out and recognized him as a master. And to them he had given this advice: 'In order for one's own words to be loved, they must belong only to oneself and not to anyone else.'

Meanwhile, apart from *Zeno*, the other books had been rescued from oblivion and, in *Senilità* especially, a successful harmonious novel had been discovered. In spite of his growing fame, discontent with himself gnawed at him, and the feeling of the little time he had to live grew ever more painful.

Summer was approaching, the last summer of his life. During the holidays, in the house at Opicina, the pages of *Il Vecchione* ('The Old Old Man') were piling up. On 16 May 1928 he had written to Benjamin Crémieux about it:

Besides, after a few less good weeks, I'm so well that, taking a sudden decision, I set out to write another novel, *Il Vec-*

chione, a continuation of *Zeno*. I wrote about 200 pages and enjoyed myself enormously. If I don't manage to finish it, it won't matter. I shall have laughed heartily once again in my life.

But even now he was not entirely free of the factory; it still held him in its tentacles with a hundred interests. So in this final part of his life he was not able to dedicate himself entirely to literature as he had always dreamed of doing.

His last letter to Signora Crémieux belongs to this period.

Trieste, 19 August 1928

Dear Good Friend,

I have received your sweet letter of 28 July and am so honoured by the news it contains that before writing to you I have had to get used to your decision. Don't think you neglected us in Paris. We had all we could reasonably expect from you and your husband and always more than we deserved. We're no longer outsiders and we know your life. In fact, I completed my study of the dogs of Paris, discovering that they don't like being looked at, because they aren't used to it. In Paris no one has the time to bother them. For us to be together, you must come to Trieste. I have so many fine things here to show you, things I'm proud of. It is true that I too am busy with my underwater paint but in special cases I make myself free of it. And there could be no more special case than the arrival of you and Signor Crémieux. Here I have been all this horrible summer between Opicina and Trieste, flattering myself that a small (small but important) piece of Paris would come and console me. As the years pass my gratitude to Signor Crémieux (and to you who – alone – encouraged me before that lazy old fellow decided to write) increases. Yesterday I laughed heartily because Borgese reproached Crémieux in the *Corriere della Sera* for not having occupied himself enough with me in his *Panorama*. That's what he needs, reproaches. Serve him right . . . for not coming to Trieste. He really doesn't take enough account of me.

In a few days I'm going off to the mountains, to Bormio (Valtellina), for a fortnight. But I shall certainly be here after 10 September, and am expecting you here on my return.

I have a terrible fear that we shall not see each other again. I no longer go to London because travelling tires me, and it will be very difficult for me to get to Paris again. The railway makes me shudder. Ten hours by car gets me to Bormio. And I realize perfectly well that we shall never meet in Trieste. Signor Crémieux managed to get out of his involvement in Romania to avoid going through Trieste, and is going to Norway instead.

You ask me what I'm thinking about. I want to write another novel, *Il Vegliardo*,[1] a continuation of *Zeno*. I've written several chapters but they'll have to be done again. A certain false note has crept into them. Can it be an old man's incapacity? If I manage to write a chapter I like, I'll send it to you.

From my wife, affectionate greetings to you and Signor Crémieux and a kiss for Francis.

As for me, I kiss your hand devotedly,

Your very affectionate

Italo Svevo.

Very high blood pressure had given him heart pains and, as in previous years, we went to Bormio for a cure, taking with us our six-year-old grandson, little Paolo. The previous year's cure had given Ettore temporary relief, so he wanted to repeat it. Our stay had been very calm, he was happy to feel the small new life growing beside him. 'How nice it is to have Ciocci with us,' he often said.

On the last day but one, while he was dressing in the room next to mine, I heard him suddenly exclaim: 'After all, I can die because I've been pretty happy.' On hearing that strange exclamation, which made an impression on me, I asked nothing, said nothing.

Until the end he had worked fervently on the novel 'The

1. Alternative title for *Il Vecchione*.

Old Old Man'. That morning he was actually writing when I called to tell him everything was ready for our departure. He abruptly interrupted his writing. His last pages are pervaded by a sense of foreboding of death. The hours that were to come are described with a hallucinatory clearness.

For women, the struggle was hopeless if religion did not support them. 'That's true,' she said, convinced of her own weakness. And yet, being full of feeling, she confessed for the first time how she had found it possible to live beside him, an atheist, without fear, 'I always prayed for you too, for you above all . . .'

And he wanted to show her that he too, in his way, had thought of her. It was for her sake that he constantly prepared himself for death. It was to be presumed he would predecease her. He needed to serve as an example to her. Religion did not always give courage . . . for the thought of death has to be that of a healthy man. That thought must be a living and strong one. Not sick. The thought of death was, for others, what prompted religion. In him it had not evolved. It had remained a simple, working religion, corresponding perfectly to every need. There was no need of heaven to make people good and merciful. The thought of death softened everything. The ardour of the struggle for life was mitigated by the decision to prepare for death.

In that light, even defeat became insignificant . . . 'Nothing seems to me as pitiful and ridiculous as the movements of an animal when the butcher's knife descends.'

Then, before going to sleep, he thought: 'Death does not threaten me. I am strong. How will she bear my death? Will she know how to imitate my resignation? But how can she feel that, in universal law, there is no place for sorrow and fear?'

Then he falls ill and the difficulty of breathing is described with real agony. His wife prayed in the darkness. Yet she knew it was utterly ignoble to kneel and ask for a miraculous intervention . . . And she found the peace she had asked for for him. The pain continued, but he spared the effort of trying to escape it. And she, for whom death finished nothing, thought, as she sought consolation for so much pain: 'Now you're having your revenge. How fine you are.'

His death was exactly the one he had not wanted: terror . . . and for a long time Teresa considered, hesitantly, the horror of that death. He had admitted to a sin: what fault? His irreligion. And she thought that at the last minute he had been converted. All that was left of Roberto on earth, that is to say in Teresa's heart, was converted. A silent conversion took place, only the fai . . .

And here the writing stopped abruptly.

The morning presaged a dark day: it was pouring with rain. However, we set off at eight, because we wanted to be at Trento before night. Our car drove towards the city, which we reached in the evening; there we stopped for the night. Next morning we set off again and at midday arrived at Treviso, where we stopped for lunch. It was still pouring with rain. I asked the chauffeur, Giovanni Colleoni, if it was not dangerous to carry on in all that rain. 'No, we go better, in fact,' he replied. Paolo, who was looking at the plan of our journey, suddenly exclaimed: 'Look, Grandma, this map finishes at Motta di Livenza.' We set off. After we had crossed the second bridge over the Livenza at Motta, the car suddenly swerved to the right. To straighten it again the chauffeur sharply turned left. The back wheels could not grip the slippery ground, and the car went zig-zagging on and collided violently with a tree. I heard Ettore shout: 'Giovanni, what are you doing?' and nothing else. When I came to, I felt a great pain in my forehead: the impact had caused a fracture in the occipital bone, and in agony I saw Paolo's face covered with a mask of blood.

Ettore, on the car floor, was groaning: 'My leg, my leg.' The chauffeur, who had remained unhurt, took him out and, as he could not stand, sat him in the road, in the rain. It was half past two in the afternoon. When, with the chauffeur's help, I was also able to get out of the car, I hastened to disinfect Paolo's cuts with the medicines from our travelling first-aid box.

Meanwhile some peasants had arrived, who ran to Motta to fetch help. A French car picked me and Paolo up; a car from Motta took Ettore. As soon as the doctor in the hospital saw us he said: 'We'll treat the worst one first,' and to my great surprise (since I was convinced that I was the most seriously injured) they took Ettore first. Then I was seized with anxiety for him. In fact, his breathlessness came on at once. It was his weak heart which could not stand the tremendous shock; the injury to his leg was not fatal.

We spent a night in hell, all three in the same room in three small beds in a row, one beside the other. Before dawn Letizia had arrived, with her husband and a nephew of ours who was a doctor, Aurelio Finzi.

In the morning Ettore's condition worsened; he could no longer bear anything. Seeing Letizia weep, he looked thoughtfully at her, and said gently: 'Don't cry, Letizia; dying is nothing.' His tongue was thick and, seeing his nephew light a cigarette, he made a sign, asking for one. Aurelio refused it. Then Ettore said, his voice already muffled: 'That would really have been the last cigarette.'

A nurse came in and asked me quietly if it was necessary to send for a priest. Although I was very religious, I said I did not think it right. Ettore heard me and I saw he was joining his hands in prayer. Trembling, I asked him: 'Ettore, do you want to pray?' 'When you haven't prayed all your life, there's no point at the last minute,' he murmured in a voice that was already fading. Then he said no more. Two hours later he was dead. It was half past two on Thursday, 13 September 1928.

Thus an accident ended his life. Our time on earth together was over. The man who had approached me as a young girl and for so many years had held me sweetly by the hand was no more. I remained alone to face the terrible storms hanging over me; alone, without his comfort, to bear the appalling horrors which the war was to pile up for our family.

WHEN I WAS BACK in Trieste I found among his papers a letter of farewell, addressed to me. It had been written seven years earlier, after my father's death:

Yesterday we buried Gioachino, and it seems important for me now, not to make my own last requests, but to make sure that after my death my lifelong companion, my wife Livia, should have a word of farewell and encouragement from me. I want her to remember, to help her in the nervous agony any death in the family causes her, how invariably sweet and loving she has been to me, and how much I always valued her sweetness and love, and lived on them. I want her to know that I am content with the affection she has given me during my life and would prefer (though I won't insist on it) for there to be no mourning and solemnity after my death. She must live as her feelings prompt her, and I want my death to confirm and enlarge her liberty, which I never willingly encroached on. In short, all I want really to do is to send her a last loving kiss. Goodbye, dear Livia. I entrust her to my son and daughter Antonio and Letizia Fonda. May she find in them all the support, respect and love she deserves: by which I mean, not that I command them thus, but that I believe it is what they will do of their free will. I send them a loving kiss also, hoping that they will never lose the love which brought them together and made Livia and me so happy. [I should like my funeral to be simple, quiet, and a *civil* one. I want to be the least trouble possible to my friends and neighbours and for things to be done in the most simple and straight-forward way, without ostentation of any kind, even of simplicity.][1]

For a long time I was ill. In the painful stupor which overwhelmed me I heard dear distant voices like warm friendly hands. Those who had the deepest understanding of Ettore were those who felt closest to me. These are some of the letters of condolence,[2] first those from the Crémieux:

1. Livia Svevo omitted these sentences from her Italian edition.
2. See 'Publisher's Note', p. viii.

'Dear Friends,

'Three lines in a French newspaper, without explanation, without a single detail, have told us that all was over, and tion in Italian newspapers, ending up almost hoping that the news was false – so eager were we not to believe it.

'In almost all of his dear letters, which we have now retrieved, put in order and re-read, there was the same appeal, which adds to our grief: "Come to Trieste, or we shall never see one another again." Why did we not take him at his word? Why did we not come this August? Why, in our journey through Tuscany, did we not give him a sign? Perhaps the disaster would have been avoided.

'Everything has been unjust in Svevo's life. Even those who, like myself, longed for an end to this injustice have not worked for it as they might have done. With that good will of his, so sweet, and satirical and full of his own special kind of resignation, he expressed gratitude for what I had done, but many times I have made him wait even for the little I did for him. I feel nothing but remorse. I knew very well, I could feel, that what he wanted even more than fame was friendship; I knew very well that he was one of those who live a life of affection, always ready to give himself to others, but needing always to feel the presence of friendly hearts.

'Of course I know what life is like, the hardness of it, which makes it so difficult to get outside oneself. But when one knows the good that one can do for another human, and that human is of the quality of Svevo, ought one not to do it?

'I can only think, in my sadness, of all that I could have done for him and did not. All the hours we could have spent together still in Paris last March and which I did not reserve for him. That trip to Trieste that we put off till next year . . .

'Neither next year, nor ever, will he be there any more . . .

'I had at least hoped that he might have died suddenly, without suffering. But no, not even that! The *Corriere* tells me that he suffered for two days. Will one of you be kind enough to tell me how he bore his last hours, and whether he was conscious of his situation?

'Dear Madame Svevo, my poor friend, I do not dare speak to you of your own injuries or tell you my wishes for your rapid recovery. What are those wounds compared with your misfortune? He is no longer with us, never again will be with us, with his slow speech, his smile, his eyes that were so vivid and so sad, always turning to you, leaning on you with the trust of a child, a great child sure of finding in you the refuge he sought. Amidst all the incomprehension from which he suffered, he was always understood, encouraged and supported by you.

'His work lives and will go on living. He lives in it himself, all complete, and one can hear there the sound of his voice, his gestures, his heart and his affectionate humour. The hour of justice has struck at last, but why need it have been the hour of death?

'How the paper I am writing on reminds me of him! That evening meeting at the PEN Club, where he was so happy, so alive, for all that he was under no illusions. He left all the other writers who were there with a charming remembrance. No one has forgotten him; they all ask for news of him every time we meet.

'The translation of *Senilità* must establish his name and his work in France for all time. I will see what I can do, I promise you.

'Dear Friends, I am ashamed of this letter which expresses what I feel so badly – that sense of unjust loss, and my own resentment and sorrow.

'I embrace you.

'B. Crémieux.'

'My Dear Great Friend,

'I cannot think what to say to express my sorrow, our consternation. I cannot believe it is all over. You will return, both of you, next Spring; or, surely, we will come and see you? Alas! that all such words and such hopes should be in vain. Yesterday evening I wrote him a last letter, I had a conversation with him; you were there too and looked on, smiling. Now when I think of you, and this will be more often than ever, I shall have to picture you alone and no longer bent over him, notebook in hand, taking down the innumerable things he confided only in you.

'How I would like to see you, dear friend, and to tell you in person of our sorrow, our deep friendship and our being with you in your triple injuries. May you quickly recover and the little child also, by thinking of him who could so little bear to see those he loved suffer.

'I embrace you sadly. Give your dear children all our friendship.

'Your Marianna Crémieux.'

The 'last letter' mentioned by Madame Crémieux had appeared in the *Nouvelles Littéraires* in September, entitled 'Adieu'.

'Dear Great Friend,

'I find myself writing to you at that table where, this Spring, with such a gay gesture, you set down a book, some flowers and a cup of tea. It seems that it will be my last letter and you will not reply, you who were always in advance in correspondence and wrote at such length. It seems that you have left Trieste for ever and that you are so far away that your shaky writing can never now reach me.

'I have collected all your letters. I have looked at them all again. Who should I consult but you yourself? I see that in every one of them there is the same plea: "Dear friend, you must both come to Trieste. If you do not come, it is clear that I shall never see you again."

'You were right! You knew. With your sweet and wise

obstinacy you were preparing for this departure, and perhaps you even knew how brutal a one it was going to be.

'And we let you go without seeing you again, you who appealed so loudly! Poor deaf people that we are! You had such need of your friends. Glory – that glory which came so late – meant a lot to you, certainly; but it was only as dear as it was to you because it was your friends who pushed you towards it. Without them it would have been an alien pleasure; you needed them in order to experience its full reality. I am sure you would have sacrificed it to them if need be.

'You loved your friends fully, ingenuously, as children love; you needed their presence; but you were so discreet and considerate that you did not ask for their presence every time you felt the need of it and you suffered yourself to do without it – suffered with such good humour. I shall never forget your air of resignation, that day this last Spring when you were leaving, you and your admirable wife. We had just been enjoying some comforting hours, all three. It was a Saturday. I said to you: "Till Tuesday", quite naturally, in the way that Parisians do at parting. But your air revealed to me that I ought to have said "Till this evening" or "Till tomorrow". No doubt I was unable to, but I ought to have dropped everything and *been* able to; for your look, in which there was no reproach, said sadly: "To be such friends; to come from so far away, at my age, for a week here, and not to see one another every day!"

'Ah! how right he was!

'Dear Italo Svevo, your book, which it took so long to open, and then to read, and then to approve, will be in all the bookshop windows now, and on every table and in everyone's hands. It is scarcely worth speaking about your work as a whole; everybody will know it and admire it; it has no need of criticism any longer, for death has done its task for it. But as for you yourself! Who will ever know the goodness of your heart, the confidence that your whole presence gave, and each of your gentle gestures! Who can know your voice, your look, the affectionate malice of your talk, in which the malice was always outweighed by the affection – your divine clumsiness, turned so cleverly against yourself, and that ardent modesty which made you like those gentle heroes, so grateful to whoever will receive the booty they bring that they end up believing quite sincerely that they are receiving what in fact they brought themselves. Like them, you sincerely believed you owed everything to your friends, but the booty was really yours, dear great man, that booty won from the thousand little wars of your troubled and patient life, those three books nourished with all your adolescence and all your youth, where the truly strong ones are like you – timid and scrupulous but in love with their own truth and with everything alive in themselves, so that they create tragedies around them, thereby amazing their companions, who believed them born only for farce.

'That smiling and lucid tragedy, that analysis of the smallest movements of consciousness, about which people have already often said that it sprang from the same ardent desire as Proust felt to pursue to the very end the infinite workings of the human heart – that almost morbid sobriety of expression, that continual terror of not being *true* enough and of writing "literature" – all those great merits of the writer, all those rare virtues of the novelist, were likewise those of the man.

'Dear Italo Svevo, you who slew all vanities, you pretended to be vain of those successes brought to you by a belated justice, and all the time you were maliciously enjoying confounding those who had not realized who you were.

'We got to know each other very quickly, thanks to the intelligence of a great friend who was the first of us who read you (Valery Larbaud), and despite some trivial hesitations.

'We exchanged great pledges of loyalty and friendship. Should I not have kept you company always? You did me the honour of believing yourself safe when I was with you. How is it that I do not keep you company today, and how shall I not voice my sorrow?

'To that desolate smile that I send to you over there, where you no longer are but where perhaps your last words are still resounding, with their slightly slow and restrained and gently persuasive Triestine accent – to that true smile of friendship, the truest of all, the one which dares express to you the admiration and tenderness that one finds so hard to express to the living – to that smile, that one alone, you will not respond, dear friend, but it will never be absent from our house.

'Marie Anne Crémieux.'

Joyce too was close to me in warm friendship:

'Paris, Sept. 24, 1928

'Dear Mrs Schmitz,

'A Trieste newspaper has been forwarded to me from Le Havre in which there is a paragraph about the fatal accident to poor Schmitz and the injuries to yourself.

'I telegraphed you at your Trieste address although I did not know where you then were.

'We are all greatly shocked to hear of his death. A very sympathetic notice by Madame Crémieux appears in the *Nouvelles Littéraires* and I am having a copy sent to you.

'I am also asking the editor of *Transition* to reprint, by permission of the same paper, Mr Nino Frank's article written when you were last here which is the best literary portrait I can recall of my old friend.[1] I, at least, can see him through the lines of it.

'Later on, when time and the remembrance of your own devotion to Italo Svevo have in some way reconciled you to such a loss, will you please let me know what success he had with the English and American publishers to whom I had recommended him?

1. Nino Frank's article, 'Un Grand Écrivain méconnu', appeared in *Nouvelles Littéraires*, 17 March 1926. It was not reprinted in *Transition*.

'I spoke to his German publisher in Zürich in July and he told me they would bring the book out this autumn.

'I hope you have recovered from your shock and your injuries. It is perhaps a poor, but still some consolation, to remember that our last meeting in Paris was so pleasant to us all.

'Please remember me if at any time my help can serve to keep alive the memory of an old friend for whom I had always affection and esteem.

'To yourself, dear Mrs Schmitz, and to your daughter, all our sympathy.

'Sincerely yours

'James Joyce.'

Giani Stuparich, who in recent years had been beside him every evening in the circle of close friends in the Caffè Garibaldi, wrote to me, deeply moved:

Trieste, 23 September 1928

'Dear and Noble Lady,

'I have let these few days of bewilderment pass before telling you about my state of mind. Even today I cannot manage to realize that Ettore Schmitz is no longer with us. In the evening I look round the Caffè, and always have a feeling that I shall see him come in, with the luminous goodness showing in his face. I came back from Florence cherishing the pleasure of seeing him again after so long – almost two months since we had met. I almost needed to hear him speak: few men opened their hearts, when they spoke, as he did. When I listened to him, although I was younger in years than he was, I felt rejuvenated by his spontaneity, his pithiness, and his eyes, which were full of knowledge and of profound inquiry, and always fresh and new as they looked at the world. What a deeply rich, genial vision he had of the human mind and what a calm, amusing happiness in reproducing aspects of life! I had known him only a few years, but meeting him was a fertile and profound experience for me, and his loss an endless regret. And I imagine what it must be for you, dear Signora, and for Signora Letizia, you who have lived day after day in the atmosphere created by his geniality and his good, generous heart.

'Believe me, I feel a little close to your inconsolable pain.
'Yours devotedly
   'Giani Stuparich.'

To his were added the voices of the young literary Italians – Valerio Jahier, Leo Ferrero, Giovanni Comisso, Alberto Tallone, Carlo Linati, and Enrico Piceni, as well as Paul-Henri Michel, Ettore's French translator, with whom he had worked in perfect harmony.

Letters also arrived from strangers who, with his great goodness, Ettore had lifted up in some dark period of their lives. Many showed regret for not having responded more warmly to his continuous longing for understanding and affection. Ettore had suffered a great deal from delays, promises long unfulfilled, and visits postponed, as if he had an obscure but precise and firmly-rooted idea of the short time still left him, and the inexorable passing of time.

Little by little I recovered; circumstances almost forced me to occupy myself with my husband's increasing fame. Letizia was entirely absorbed in her family, and among our relations all the men were attracted to the world of business.

Many special numbers of periodicals were dedicated to Ettore's memory. In February 1929 the *Convegno* appeared, with articles by Giacomo Debenedetti, Carlo Linati, Giani Stuparich and Alberto Rossi; and in April the number of *Solaria* was dedicated to him, with more than thirty articles by writers, Italian and foreign: G. B. Angioletti, Marcel Brion, Jacques Boulanger, Juan Chabas, Alberto Consiglio, Benjamin Crémieux, Giacomo Debenedetti, Ilya Ehrenburg, Giansiro Ferrata, Raffaello Franchi, Piero Gadda, Ivan Goll, Franz Hellens, James Joyce, Valery Larbaud, C.V.

Lodovici, Aldo Pallazzeschi, Giuseppe Raimondi, Albertc Rossi, Umberto Saba, Ernst Schwenk, Sergio Solmi, Philippe Soupault, Giani Stuparich, Bonaventura Tecchi, Arthur Van Schendel, André Thérive. Here are some pencilled notes which bring it alive to me again:

Giacomo Debenedetti recalls a visit to Villa Veneziani and describes Ettore's way of speaking, which suggests to him the image of a spider weaving at the centre of his subtle web. Ivan Goll calls him the old great uncle who, when he dies, leaves a rich inheritance to his nephews in literature. They shall not be disappointed.

Valery Larbaud reveals the Triestine character and Trieste itself: 'Where a disenchanted comic muse, subtle and kind, dwelt for some time.'

C.V. Lodovici recalls a meeting in Milan in the editorial office of a periodical. 'I found him already talking in that "socratic" voice of his. His bearing was English rather than Saxon, with Mediterranean clothes, sweetness in his language and clear, humorous goodness in his expression.'

Enzo Ferrieri too, in the *Convegno* number dedicated to his memory, described him thus: 'As soon as he came to Milan he would come and see us, and in the evening everyone would come along and toast our guest, who so much enjoyed being toasted. This seemed to make him happy. If he sat at the head of the table the evenings were always friendly, and the conversation, with his intellectual and worldly bonhomie, could never go wrong.'

NEWSPAPER CUTTINGS came to me, in every language and from every part of the world. Every morning I awaited them with the same anxious joy he had known.

One day I decided to examine his papers. I went into his small study, where Veruda's paintings still looked down from the walls and the violin was silent; and there, among the simple pieces of furniture, where he had thought and written so much, I settled down in a mood of calm expectancy.

I found everything in great disorder, letters jumbled with
unpublished work, notes for the last novel mixed with
thoughts and plays. These papers reflected the absorbed,
absent-minded man he had always been. I divided everything
tidily into files. Thus, after his death, I continued to help him
with the precision and orderliness that were so much a part of
my nature. The large number of unpublished works surprised me. There were many fables, short dialogues which he
used to embody his profound human philosophy, and all his
plays: those of his youth, begun while Elio waited anxiously
for them, and the later ones. The early ones bore the
pseudonym E. Samigli. There were light comedies: *Le Teorie
del Conte Alberto* (*The Theories of Count Alberto*), *Le Ire di
Giuliano* (*The Anger of Giuliano*), *La Verità* (*Truth*), and even
a sketch in dialect, untitled. The other works were later,
deeper and more complex: *L'Avventura di Maria* (*Maria's
Adventure*) and *A Husband*, which he had particularly loved
and had dreamed of seeing on the stage.

The latter, which was rather long, was not so much a play
as a long story in dialogue, and perhaps a prelude, with the
same characters, to the unfinished 'The Old Old Man'.
Among the many manuscripts of short stories were 'Mariano
da Venezia', which deals with the strange figure of a workman of ours in the factory at Murano, and 'Passeggiate in
Friuli' ('Walks in Friuli'), in which he described a type of
peasant we knew.

Reading 'Umbertino' I found once again the world of
childhood he had gazed at with so much curiosity in Letizia's
sons and his nephew Umbertino, and treated with delicate
touches. In 'Argo e il suo padrone' ('Argo and His Master'), I
found again his faithful affection for dogs. He had loved
birds, too. The sparrows which flew round our house looking
for food distracted him. The longest manuscript, entitled
Corto Viaggo Sentimentale (*Short Sentimental Journey*), consisted of a collection of types and impressions gathered on the
journey between Milan and Venice. He had written it in the

period between *The Confessions of Zeno* and 'The Old Old Man'. One uncompleted story was called 'Il Malocchio' ('The Evil Eye'). Among the papers of his young days was an essay, 'Del Sentimento in Arte' ('On Feeling in Art'). The pages were covered with his writing, which was then larger and clearer, almost more formally correct than it later became. Then there was still his lecture on James Joyce and the various sketches for 'The Old Old Man', written in an old man's hand, which was weaker and more uneven.

We decided as a family to collect several stories and the last pages of the interrupted novel in a single volume and, less than a year after Ettore's death, in April 1929, this posthumous volume appeared, published by Morreale. 'The Story of the Nice Old Man and the Pretty Girl and Other Works' had an introductory note by Eugenio Montale: 'Among Svevo's papers,' he wrote, 'we find minor works, not yet *nugae*; and in this case they are closely linked with major works and show an inner activity, a ferment of surprising development.'

The book had a good press. Young Italian critics welcomed it with understanding and excitement; Linati, Debenedetti, Vittorini, and Franchi wrote about it. Silvio Benco wrote: 'The pages of "The Old Old Man" which have been found (I am not speaking of those at the note-stage) could easily be the beginning of a masterpiece. They are among the finest and most illuminating that Svevo ever wrote; densest in thought, most responsive to the intensity of his observation. If it had been completed, the novel might have been his major work.'

The first critical study of him in book form, *L'opera di Italo Svevo*, appeared in the winter of 1928. It was by the Triestine writer Federico Sternberg, professor of German literature at the University of Turin, who had a long-standing brotherly friendship with my husband. Ettore had read and approved the unpublished work – which he nonetheless said was too laudatory. Sternberg had also organized the official com-

memoration at the most important cultural society in Trieste,
the Minerva, honouring the memory of one of Trieste's
greatest sons, indeed, the only one to achieve world fame. In
February 1929, Sternberg published another book, *L'arte e
la personalità di Italo Svevo*.

On 26 April 1931, a bronze was unveiled in the public
gardens, the work of the Triestine sculptor Giovanni Mayer,
which we had presented to the city. Among the greenery, not
far from the bronze image of his early friend, Umberto
Veruda, in that same garden in which the characters of his
novels unburdened their passions, and where the two friends
discussed the artistic dreams which tormented their souls,
Ettore seems to be smiling. In 1954, in a solemn ceremony,
the Society of Art and Culture presented another bronze bust
of Italo Svevo, the work of the sculptor Ruggero Rovan, to
the University of Trieste.

Meanwhile, Piero Rismondo's German translation of *Zeno*
appeared, published by Rhein-Verlag. Ettore had dealt with
the publishing firm Joyce had suggested to him, and which
had also published the translation of *Ulysses*. He had known
the young translator, and had exchanged lively letters with
him. In one of the last he had begged him to hurry and
publish his *Zeno* in German, 'because I am afraid of dying'.

From France and Germany, his fame spread to England
and the great English public at last approached him, the
people he had observed during his long stays in London,
without imagining that they would one day honour him so
highly. A young English writer, Beryl de Zoete, wrote to me,
suggesting herself as translator. I went to London and we
met. She had already translated 'A Hoax'. For the publication I dealt with the Hogarth Press, a director of which was
the husband of the great writer Virginia Woolf. 'Generous
Wine' was published in English – as 'The Wine that Kindles'
– in the American review *Transition* in Paris. Beryl de Zoete
also found a publisher for *Zeno*.[1] In 1930 the English and

1. Putnam & Co. Ltd, London and New York.

American editions of it appeared. It was triumphantly successful, particularly in America. Soon afterwards there followed the English translation of 'The Story of the Nice Old Man and the Pretty Girl'. In May 1929 I met Marcel Thiébaut, director of the firm of Calmann-Lévy in Paris; through Paul-Henri Michel he had suggested to me the publication of *As a Man Grows Older* in French. We came to an agreement, and dear Michel set to work with enthusiasm. The book came out in 1930, and in 1932 the English edition, for England and America, appeared.

The German literary world also took an increasing interest in Svevo's work. Dr Karl Hellwig wrote to ask me about the German translation of 'The Old Old Man', which appeared in 1930 in the *Neue Schweizer Rundschau*, followed immediately by the story 'The Mother' in the *Neues Wiener Journal*. In 1932 the German translation of a group of stories, with a preface by the translator, Karl Hellwig, appeared in Berlin in one volume.

During a visit to Spain I met Juan Chabas, who in 1927 and 1928 had translated 'Generous Wine' and an extract from *Zeno*, and had published them in Spanish journals. He told me he would like to translate all my husband's works into Spanish, and I agreed that he should. I wanted a contract with the publisher Juventud, of Barcelona, but the stormy political events in Spain made this impossible, and in any case the translator did not at the time manage to finish the work he had begun. The publishers Ediciones Aymo, of Barcelona, with whom I had a contract in August 1942 for the publication in Spanish of all the novels, told me in 1945 that Franco's government had forbidden the publication of *The Confessions of Zeno*.

Those were years of work and of intense enthusiasm. Ettore's fame spread from England to America, and from Spain to the Balkans. Antonio Nizeteo, a Dalmatian, translated *As a Man Grows Older* into Croatian, and published it in Zagreb. A Polish edition of *The Confessions of*

Zeno also appeared, and I signed contracts with publishers in Holland and Denmark.

I waited anxiously for cuttings from newspapers and reviews, which came to me from every country and language. He too had waited for the post each morning, which confirmed the fact that he was alive in the world. I arranged the cuttings and catalogued them very carefully, as if I must one day render an account to him. I also brought out a book of extracts of the critics' most salient points. My suffering was thus softened a little, and my great loneliness was helped. I felt I was a custodian of his fame and had a task to carry out; I dreamed of the publication of his complete works.[1]

The praise in the newspapers, and my contact with young writers of the new literary generation who came to Trieste from many countries to find Svevo's home, gave me great pleasure. These writers asked if as a great favour they might study his papers, and reverently examined the manuscripts and unpublished works in his study, and consulted the criticisms. After several months I used to receive their theses.

1. Svevo's *Opera omnia*, edited by Bruno Maier, was published in six volumes (Dall'Oglio, Milan, 1966–78) as follows: I. *Epistolario*, 1966; II. *Romanzi*, 1969; III. *Racconti, saggi e pagine sparse*, 1968; IV. *Commedie*, 1969; V. *Lettere a Svevo. Diario di Elio Schmitz*, 1973; VI. *Carteggio con James Joyce, Valéry Larbaud, Benjamin Crémieux, Marie-Anne Comnène, Eugenio Montale, Valerio Jahier*, 1978. This edition will eventually be replaced by a critical edition now being published by Studio Tesi, Pordenone, under the editorship of Bruno Maier, of which the following volumes have so far appeared: *Una Vita* (1985), *La Coscienza di Zeno* (1985), *Senilità* (1986), *Il Vegliardo* (1987).

In English there is a five-volume selected Uniform Edition (Secker & Warburg, 1962–9) as follows: 1. *The Confessions of Zeno*, translated by Beryl de Zoete (1962); 2. *As a Man Grows Older*, translated by Beryl de Zoete (1962); 3. *A Life*, translated by Archibald Colquhoun (1963); 4. *Short Sentimental Journey and Other Stories* ('The Hoax', 'The Story of the Nice Old Man and the Pretty Girl', 'Generous Wine', 'Traitorously', 'Argo and His Master', 'The Mother', 'Short Sentimental Journey', 'Death'), translated by Beryl de Zoete, L. Collison-Morley and Ben Johnson (1967); 5. *Further Confessions of Zeno* ('The Old Old Man', 'An Old Man's Confessions', 'Umbertino', 'A Contract', 'This Indolence of Mine', *Regeneration: a Comedy in three Acts*), translated by Ben Johnson and P.N. Furbank (1969).

The first was that of a student from Pirano in Istria, Maria Punter, who was studying at Pisa University; then came that of Maria Rosa Pescio from Genoa and, from faraway California, that of Edward Sellards, studying at the Sorbonne in Paris. Maria Borsatti from Bucharest University, Niní Badaracco from Milan, and Alfonso della Rocca from Naples also sent their theses, and the last I heard about was that of Luigia Zenni, from Rome.

Periodicals often asked for unpublished works. After I had given them groups of my husband's fables, I thought of the plays which had been very dear to him and formed a part of his literary activity almost unknown to the public. It was the *Convegno* in Milan which first published, in 1931, *A Husband*, written in 1903, and later, in 1937, *Maria's Adventure*. In 1932 *La Panarie* of Udine published the one-act tragedy *Inferiorità*.

Without my knowing it, a small book appeared in Trieste in 1932 containing an unknown play of Ettore's, which had not been among his papers even in the form of a sketch: *Il Ladro in Casa* ('The Thief in the House'). It was published under the auspices of the Triestine dialect poet Piazzetta [Giulio Piazza], who must have received it as a gift from my husband. Still unpublished are 'The Theories of Count Alberto', 'Le Ire di Giuliano' ('Giuliano's Anger') an early work, 'La Parola' ('The Word') and 'Truth', as well as a play in dialect and some unfinished pieces.

When admirers wanted to stand near his grave, I would take them to the large, white, flower-filled cemetery of Sant'Anna, not far from the sea. There I would open the gate of the chapel, built in the form of a small temple, where the dead of my family are gathered. On the wall to the left of the altar, on which Sassoferrato's gentle madonna is shown in Florentine mosaics, there is the inscription: 'Ettore Schmitz (Italo Svevo) 19 December 1861–13 September 1928'. Beneath it is a low relief by the sculptor Mayer, which shows him looking thoughtful and a little stern.

Here he rests in the arms of the mystery on which he had meditated for so long. He will, I hope, have found the peace he never achieved in his soul, and overcome the horror of the unknown which made him write on a piece of paper: 'The time will come when man no longer fears dying.'

Here is his final home, the last that is left; for the serene and peaceful Villa Veneziani, with its green shutters, its pergola covered in wistaria, its large music-room and its glass verandah, was crushed by the onslaught of incendiary and high-explosive bombs on 20 February 1945. Only part of the front remains standing, like an empty, smoky stage-set, bearing witness to the house which once contained so much energy and so many lives.

Vanished forever is the small study where Ettore's desk was, and the music stand for his violin, vanished the shrine where I kept all his unpublished works, vanished all the fine editions of books translated into so many languages, watched over by Veruda's large paintings, in which the figures took on an intensity of life which varied according to the light. The peaceful home enlivened by the laughter of our small grandsons no longer exists. They too paid their share in a terrible destiny of suffering: Piero and Paolo were taken prisoner in Russia in January 1943, and both died of their privations in March the same year; and Sergio, the youngest, the most like his grandfather in the breadth of his brow, the sweetness of his smile, and the thoughtful mind drawn to meditation and art, died fighting for freedom, shot by the Germans in a Trieste street on the morning of the city's uprising on 1 May 1945, while his father, Colonel Fonda Savio, was directing the uprising from his command post.

All Ettore's works have survived, including those still unpublished. In August 1943, buffeted by the storm of racial persecution, I fled from Trieste to Arcade, in the province of Treviso, taking them with me to safety. Letizia and Sergio came with me, and in a large, carefully guarded trunk, we took with us the manuscripts, letters, unpublished pieces, books and translations. Thus the part of his work which must still see the light was saved.

At the end of the war I was able to have my first contacts with a free Italy, and in May 1945 I received the first number of the journal *Il Mondo*, edited by Alessandro Bonsanti, which published the first draft of 'Short Sentimental Journey', with an introduction by Umbro Apollonio whom, in 1943, I had put in charge of the unpublished works. Thus when Italy was liberated, one of the first to be honoured was Svevo, over whom the last years had thrown a cloak of silence, a silence occasionally broken by outbursts from the younger critics and writers. As soon as they appeared, new periodicals asked me insistently for his unpublished work. *Mondo Europeo* published 'Orazio Cima', the periodical *Costume* 'Mariano da Venezia' and the *Briarcliff Quarterly* 'Generous Wine', under the title 'Heady Wine'.

More requests came from America, too. Professor Renato Poggioli of Harvard asked for the letters and was particularly interested in the correspondence with Joyce.

The year 1947 saw the fourth edition of *The Confessions of Zeno*, with an important study by Silvio Benco; 1949, the fourth edition of *As a Man Grows Older*.

As early as 1942 I had begun to collect these memories, with the help of Lina Galli. They were to be my contribution to an understanding of Svevo, for I am convinced that knowledge of an artist's life allows a deeper penetration into his mystery.

The characters his spirit created are still alive and vital all over the world, but the three proud saplings descended from him lie in the silence of death, cut off by the terrible war: Piero and Paolo in unknown graves in Russia, Sergio in the white cemetery of our native city, not far from his grandfather's grave.

Letizia and I live on memories, until the day when Ettore, with his grandsons around him, welcomes us at the gates of eternity.

JAMES JOYCE

BY ITALO SVEVO

TRANSLATED BY STANISLAUS JOYCE

NOTE ON THE TRANSLATION

The timbre of Stanislaus Joyce's educated Dublin voice adds, in his translation, to the colour and authenticity of the Triestine timbre with which 'Italo Svevo' delivered his tribute – in a lecture given in Milan in 1927 – to Stanislaus's brother James. Stanislaus himself was no mean stylist, and his translation gives us the tone of those countless English lessons given by the Joyce brothers in the Schmitz household, and the atmosphere of the Joyce household itself. But if he has a translator's flair, often fully matching his original, he also has some translator's vices, including some outright lapses which, for the sake of fidelity to what Svevo actually said about James Joyce, have been corrected in this edition. Likewise where he thinks fit to improve on Svevo's text, as in making Svevo refer to 'Jim' instead of 'Joyce', quite against the tone of the real relationship between the two writers; or when he changes Svevo's judgement on Joyce's tastes in music from 'eclectic' to 'fastidious'. Literary sleuths can track down these amendments against the text of Stanislaus Joyce's translation (New Directions, New York, 1950) and the original Italian reprinted in Italo Svevo, *Scritti su Joyce*, edited by Giancarlo Mazzacurati (Pratiche, Parma, 1986, pp. 45–75).

JOHN GATT-RUTTER

JAMES JOYCE CAME to Trieste in October of 1904.[1] He did so by chance. He was looking for a situation and he found one in the Berlitz School in our city after a stay of a few months in Pola. It was not a very good job; but when he arrived in Trieste, he had in his pockets, besides the small sum necessary for his long journey, various manuscripts: most of the lyrics that were to be published in the volume entitled *Chamber Music*, and some of the stories of *Dubliners*. All his other works down to *Ulysses* were born in Trieste. *Chamber Music* was published in 1907, *Dubliners* in 1914, and *Stephen Dedalus* (as the French title reads), or, to give it its proper title, *A Portrait of the Artist as a Young Man*, bears the double date Dublin, 1904– Trieste, 1914. Even part of *Ulysses* was born in the shadow of San Giusto, for Joyce lived amongst us for several months after the war. In 1921 I was asked to bring him his notes for the last episode from Trieste to Paris. They amounted to a few pounds of loose sheets, which I was chary of touching lest I should upset an order that seemed to me unstable.

In 1904, when about to leave Dublin, Joyce married, and his two children were born at Trieste, so one can understand that we Triestines have a right to regard him with deep affection as if he belonged in a certain sense to us. And as if he were to a certain extent Italian. In Joyce's culture there is a marked Italian bias, accentuated by the desire, which was very lively at some periods of his life, to feel less English. In *Ulysses*, whenever it suits him, he makes free use of some of our racy turns of speech, leaving the English reader, if he is curious on the point, to get out his Italian dictionary. It is a great title of honour for my city that in *Ulysses* some of the streets of Dublin stretch on and on into the windings of our old Trieste. Recently Joyce wrote to me: 'If Anna Livia (the Liffey) were not swallowed up by the Ocean, she would certainly debouch into the Canal Grande of Trieste.'

1. Svevo has September 1903. In fact James Joyce first came to Trieste in March 1905, then returned more permanently in March 1907. Svevo met him later that year [J.G-R.]

In his lively mind points of contact between the two cities were certainly established. That could easily be: Trieste was for him a little Ireland which he was able to contemplate with more detachment than he could his own country. To the Irish critic Boyd,[1] who asserted that *Ulysses* was merely the product of pre-war thought in Ireland, Valery Larbaud replied, 'Yes, in so far as it came to maturity in Trieste.'

In retrospect – and I love to make this boast – his sojourn at Trieste is for Joyce a very sweet memory. At times there was regret. Perhaps such regret was the origin of his well-known drama *Exiles*. 'Exiled?' I asked when I was present at the performance of the play by the Stage Society in London. 'Exiled? People who return to their home country!' 'But don't you remember,' said Joyce to me, 'how the prodigal son was received by his brother in his father's house. It is dangerous to leave one's country, but still more dangerous to go back to it, for then your fellow-countrymen, if they can, will drive a knife into your heart.'

When on arriving in Paris after a long absence from my own country, I go to call on Joyce in his nice quiet flat in the Square Robiac, I seem to be returning home. Mrs Joyce, too, is deeply attached to the country in which she together with her husband spent the best years of her life. Happy years, although his later years have been richer in comforts and coloured with what is best in the life of Paris.

Yes! The author who is known to the public for being loose and licentious is a decent father of a family. I remember that when Joyce was so annoyed about the burning of his book *Dubliners*, he said to me: 'What is certain is that I am more virtuous than all that lot – I, who am a real monogamist and have never loved but once in my life.'

Joyce knew our language and literature before arriving in Trieste. I know an article[2] by the then eighteen-year-old Joyce in which Giordano Bruno, the Nolan, is quoted. In the same article there is a passage which is an evident imitation of Dante. He says: 'There are two great living dramatists, Ibsen

1. Ernest Boyd, author of *Ireland's Literary Renaissance* (1916) [J.G-R.]
2. 'The Day of the Rabblement', privately published in 1901 [J.G-R.]

and Hauptmann, and the third shall not be wanting when his hour comes. Even now that hour may be standing by the door.' A real translation into modern flesh and blood such as he was later to attempt to do with Homer.

The quotation from the Nolan is worthy of note because it sounds like an announcement of a purpose made by this youth, a purpose to which he was always faithfully to adhere in his maturity. As I am not very familiar with the works of Giordano Bruno, I shall translate it from the English: 'No man, said the Nolan, can be a lover of the true or the good unless he abhors the multitude; and the artist, though he may employ the crowd, is very careful to isolate himself.'

Thus was Stephen Dedalus born, to whom in *Ulysses* the name of Telemachus (far from the struggle) was to be attributed. Thus too, I must add, was James Joyce born, the law of whose life was to be aristocratic solitude. A goodly measure of independence and – let me put it more bluntly – of arrogance accompanied him along the paths he was to travel alone, judged and restrained by no one.

That answer of his to an elder Irish poet must belong to this period of his youth: 'I admit that you have had no influence whatever on me, but it is deplorable that you are too old to feel mine.'

The firm consciousness of his own strength, which could still only be latent in so young a man, fills me with astonishment. If I had read that article in 1901, when it was written, I should have laughed at it. Now it makes me think. So the sapling in the nursery can know that it is to become a tall pine.

In appearance Joyce has not changed much from what he was when he arrived in Trieste. He is over forty. Lean, lithe, tall, he might almost seem a sportsman if he had not the negligent gait of a person who does not care what he does with his limbs.

I believe I am right in thinking that those limbs have been very much neglected and that they have never known either sport or gymnastics. What I mean is that from near he does not give the impression of being the tough fighter that his courageous work would lead you to expect. He is very shortsighted and wears strong glasses that make his eyes look enlarged. Those eyes are blue and very notable even without the glasses, and they gaze with a look of ceaseless curiosity matched with supreme coldness. I cannot help imagining that Joyce's eye would rest no less curiously and no less coldly on any adversary with whom he might have an encounter. It must be because I see him so seldom and think of him so much.

After reading *Ulysses* there can be no doubt that his nose is not so refined, but his ear is that of a poet and musician. I know that when Joyce has written a page of prose he thinks that he has paralleled some page of music that he delights in. This feeling – I cannot say whether it accompanies his inspiration because I only know that it follows it – proves his desire. In regard to music he is oddly eclectic. He understands the German classics, old Italian music, popular music where he comes across it, Richard Wagner, even our composers of operas from Spontini down, and the Frenchmen as far as Debussy. He possesses a magnificent tenor voice; and one who loves him hoped for a long time to see him tread the boards triumphantly, made up as Faust or Manrico. Even now Mrs Joyce regrets that her husband preferred the art that has made him one of the best known and most hated men in that Anglo-Saxon world to which he unwillingly belongs.

His eclecticism in music leads him to throw his arms wide open to the future. Last year Mlle Monnier of the *Navire d'Argent* gathered some cultured musicians together one evening to hear the latest thing in modern music by an American composer, Anthil or Antheil.[1] After a quarter of an hour of it many of the guests rose and went away, protesting and wailing. But Joyce declared, 'He reminds me of Mozart.' I cannot doubt Joyce's sincerity. He had attempted, and perhaps succeeded in the attempt, to superimpose on that

1. Georges Antheil, who styled himself, in the title of his autobiography, *The Bad Boy of Music* [J.G-R.]

music some literary dream of his own. Of course the connection between literature and music cannot be wholly musical because it is also literary.

Joyce's outward life at Trieste can be summed up as a spirited struggle to support his family. His inner life was complex but already clear-cut: the elaboration of the subject matter offered him by his childhood and youth. A piece of Ireland was ripening under our sun. But the struggle cost him dear; for the life of a gerund-monger is not an easy one.

It was not until after the war that success relieved him of every preoccupation. Sometimes he strove to make his life at Trieste easier either by seeking advancement in his profession or by changing it. On one occasion he sat an examination to compete for a professorship at Padua University in English.[1] I do not know how it came about, but what is certain is that he did not get the job, and I shall never forget his disappointment. On another occasion he learned that in his native city Dublin there was not a single motion picture theatre while Trieste was swarming with them. He persuaded a cinema proprietor to open a branch in Dublin, and even went over himself to help the foreigners find their way around in John Bull's other island. He was to have shared in the profits. Unfortunately there were no profits, and the whole group came home again a little out of pocket. Joyce also contributed articles to a newspaper and was English correspondent in a bank. He did not lack friends in Trieste. The little foreign poet with his culture, his originality, and his wit, brought into our group an agreeable note which was very surprising and charming. Then he translated into Italian an Irish drama, *Riders to the Sea*, which takes place in a tragic country, a hill on a little island in the Atlantic, whose waves dash against the base of the hill and sometimes rise and sweep away people and things. Joyce tried to preserve in his translation something of the old-world dialect that is still spoken there. Nobody was prepared to produce it. It might be said, in fact, that Joyce wasted a lot of time. But, says

1. In fact, for a school-teaching certificate [J.G-R.]

Stephen Dedalus in *Ulysses*, 'a man of genius makes no mistakes. His errors are volitional and are the portals of discovery.' This is said in reference to Shakespeare, who married a woman older than himself, who proved unfaithful to him according to Dedalus of the wicked tongue. And so that you may not miss one of Joyce's good gibes, I must tell you how this capricious line of thought continues, 'Portals of discovery opened to let in the quaker librarian, softcreak-footed, bald, eared and assiduous.'

Whenever you read a biographical notice of Joyce, you find definitely stated that he never took any share in his country's struggles; and that in his *Ulysses* the part of Telemachus (far from the struggle) is appropriately given to the character who most resembles him. On the contrary, Joyce took part in those struggles from afar, from Trieste, with two articles in the *Piccolo della Sera*. The second of these, which appeared on 16 May 1912, is magnificent in its indignation and irony. I shall read you the end of it, not so much to let you hear the Italian prose of a great English writer as to give you an exact idea of the attitude of citizen Joyce (an attitude which it seems to me has its importance if we want to understand the writer), and so that the idea will be more exact than if I were to give it in my own words. 'In his last proud appeal to the Irish people Parnell implored them not to throw him to the English wolves that were howling around him. It reflects honour on his countrymen that they did not fail his desperate appeal. They did not throw him to the English wolves: they tore him to pieces themselves.' Here you see Joyce walking through the world with one sole comrade in faith, Parnell. And Parnell is dead. Our poet here, it seems, is Zarathustra carrying the great man's corpse on his back.

He is twice a rebel, against England and against Ireland. He hates England and would like to transform Ireland. Yet he belongs so much to England that like a great many of his Irish predecessors he will fill pages of English literary history and not the least splendid ones; and he is so Irish that the English have no love for him. They are out of sympathy with

him, and there is no doubt that his success could never have
been achieved in England if France and some literary Americans had not imposed it. Another Irishman, Bernard Shaw, found the solution of the problem in the readiness of great wit. He abused the English and they applauded him. It is an easy way to hit it off together. But Shaw, except for his hatred of English political history, is a true-born Briton by education. If he wanted to waste his time, he could become an English Labour Prime Minister with perfect political sincerity. And the upshot is that his relations with the English people are not much unlike those of one of our great poets with us. The more he despised us, the louder swelled our applause. Well, and what about it? We felt we were applauding ourselves.

There may be a suspicion that something of this hatred of Joyce's affects even the delicate instrument that stands him in such good stead, and which he should revere: the English language – brief and nervous by nature, and in his hands as swift and obedient as a thoroughbred. There is an episode in *Ulysses* in which something is told repeatedly in a pattern of concentric circles, as it were. It is narrated in nine cycles, and Joyce uses for each of them the language of a certain period. At first pure Anglo-Saxon; then the language undergoes the strange adventures of Latin and French influences. Later it becomes Teutonic again with Chaucer and Shakespeare, and so on down to our times, represented by the prose of Cardinal Newman. But right after, as if in mockery, comes an ugly American dialect – an evolution ending in disaster.

In 1907, at Trieste, Joyce was awaiting the publication of *Chamber Music* but not with the pleasant expectation of a writer who is waiting to see the final expression of his thought made public. It no longer seemed to him to be what he really felt and thought. In a drawer of his desk the stories of *Dubliners*, the first steps along the road that was to lead him so far, were piling up. He wanted to send off a telegram to the publisher to hold up the publication. It was his brother Stan who prevented him from doing so. And he was right. *Chamber Music* helps to throw light on the author of *Ulysses*.

The success was greater than the author had expected. Some serious critics, Arthur Symons among the first (I am quoting from Larbaud), discovered that those verses which appeared in such a modest guise revived a glorious lyrical tradition, that of the songs of the Elizabethan era, a glory too easily forgotten because it was overshadowed at its birth by the incomparable splendour of the English tragic poets. It seemed as if a poet of that age had come to life again. Now I can explain this strange fact. There is no question of imitation. Much of Joyce's youth was agitated by doubt as to which was the language of his race. A return to Gaelic? That was difficult. So instead the youth lived over again and loved the language and metres of the first conquerors. Beyond that he could not go. Sometime ago an English actor declared that to render English life of a bygone age intelligible to his audience he was obliged, in making a Shakespearian pun, to imitate the pronunciation that he found intact in Galway. I thought of Joyce at once: Joyce's poems have been included in various anthologies, and recited, and many of them set to music. Joyce was astonished. He had given proof of his very great virtuosity.

You are acquainted with *Dubliners*. Recently Eugenio Montale contributed an exhaustive study of the book to the *Fiera Letteraria*. The importance of these stories has paled in comparison with the works that followed them, but we may say that what is fundamental in Joyce can be found entire in them. He is the objective narrator who neglects nothing and forgets nothing, not a line, not a colour. You can lay your hand on his characters. True, we sometimes jostle people on the footpath who get in our way and whom we remember chiefly if they tread on our toes. Many of Joyce's characters traipse about that way and hurt us. Even Larbaud has recognized that they are slight creatures worthy only to appear as extras on the stage with the princely characters that were to people Joyce's novels.

These stories are very different from those of Maupassant, who can give us a whole life-story in a nutshell. In these, just so much of a life-story goes into the nutshell as will fit in.

Joyce's cleverness is such that we do not feel the wrench, and
we are left with the impression that we have had our proper
ration.

In the Anglo-Saxon world these stories of *Dubliners*, which
in our country or in France would have been admired and
received with equanimity, provoked a scandal which ended
in 1912 with the book's being burnt by the publisher. When
Joyce left Dublin to come back to Trieste, he could not
conclude his journey without taking revenge. From Holland
he sent back to Ireland a broadsheet of verses in which the
publisher is made to speak, and confesses to have printed a
'quite illegible railway guide'.[1] Joyce aimed at the heart of the
businessman who had wounded him to the heart.

I was always much amused by Joyce's indignation at the
misadventures that befell him. He writes with complete
freedom, as everybody knows, and in English, and yet he is
surprised at the reaction his work produces. It is proof of his
perfect good faith. With us, discussions on this subject
belong to the blessed time of my youth, but I fear that if
Ulysses were translated here such discussions would be
revived. In Joyce there is no pornography in the real sense of
the word. Those descriptions of his which are deplored
arouse disgust in quite a different way from those of his
naturalist predecessors. His biographer, Herbert Gorman,
thinks that as Joyce broke away with an immense effort from
an ethical system, he rebelled at the same time against
traditional codes and customs. That may be all the more true
if we bear in mind that Joyce was driven by his fate into many
rebellions in order to succeed in being himself. Larbaud
thinks that Joyce's disconcerting liberty of expression is due
to the influence of the great Jesuit casuists, Escobar and
Father Sanchez. The English turn up their noses, remembering that many Irishmen have the same failing: Swift, Moore
and Synge. It is certain that if *Ulysses* were purged of certain
words and of certain whole episodes, it would no longer be
what it is. It must be accepted or rejected as a whole.

1. 'Gas from a Burner', a broadside against the publisher George
Roberts, privately printed in Trieste in 1912 [J.G-R.]

The danger with which, in my view, Joyce's cleverness threatened him was obviated by a kind fate which led him at the beginning of his career to tell in *A Portrait of the Artist as a Young Man* the story of his youth. I recognize that this novel is not a real autobiography. I am informed of the fact by those who have written about it and who have had daily intercourse with Joyce. But neither is Goethe's, though he most assuredly began it with the intention of making it one. When an artist remembers, he creates at the same time. But one's own personality, upon which the whole process of creation hinges, is a very important part of life and very close to one, and no cleverness can falsify it. I would say that in the process of inspiration it changes because it becomes more complete. It is a vast experiment. Listen to what Dedalus says about it in *Ulysses*: 'As we, or mother Dana, weave and unweave our bodies, from day to day, then molecules shuttled to and fro, so does the artist weave and unweave his image.'

Everybody who knows Joyce knows that the Joyce who washes himself every day is not Stephen Dedalus, the unwashed bard, who thinks when he sees others washing and scratching themselves: 'They are trying to get at their consciences.' Dedalus is loose-spoken, while Joyce one day called me to task because I allowed myself to make a rather free joke. 'I never say that kind of thing,' said he, 'though I write it.' So it seems that his own books cannot be read in his presence. Perhaps some other personage has stolen into Dedalus; but it is all so welded together, so much of a piece, that as in cabinet-making it is impossible to see the juncture of the added piece. It is, however, the autobiography of Joyce the artist. If it were not, it would be necessary to believe that at that time Dublin hatched another artist of the same calibre, which I doubt very much. In fact, it is part of the novelty of the work that it makes the reader feel he is watching the evolution of an artist, and of an artist of importance. The tragedy of the book lies in the doubt whether in such circumstances the artist will succeed in emitting his lusty breath or die strangled. For the rest, Joyce

signed his first published writings with the name Stephen
Dedalus. It is a confession.

A Portrait of the Artist as a Young Man could be inserted in *Ulysses* as one of the chapters if the manner in which the subject is presented did not characterize it as a thing apart. I consider it a kind of preface. Fate has assigned to it the place of a preface, a very notable preface, however, which has shown that it is able to live its own independent and glorious life. But the importance of *Ulysses* is now so great that in this first novel we see and hear chiefly those elements which are a preparation for the second and a commentary on it. Without knowing the whole story of the religious and artistic evolution of Dedalus one cannot thoroughly understand *Ulysses*. As a child he is entrusted to the care of the Jesuits. Already he is marked out to be an artist and no education can obliterate that hallmark. See how his whole soul responds to the news of Parnell's death. He is ten years of age, just the age Joyce was at the time; and for him Parnell is an important person because whenever his name is mentioned, home becomes like all the rest of Ireland, and violent squabbles break out in it. He is ill in the infirmary, and it seems to him that the announcement of Parnell's death comes from the sea, shouted by one of the Jesuit fathers from aboard a steamer entering port to the people assembled on the shore. Perhaps it was fever that caused the vision, but it was the fever of an ingenuous artist who, besides imagining the great sea and the ship's arrival, entrusted the announcement to the most important person he knew.

The intellectual life of Stephen's childhood is happy and unclouded. Joyce still feels admiration and gratitude for the care of his educators, whilst his stern Dedalus cannot find time to say so. He grows up free enough. When he reaches the age at which one begins to form an opinion of the writers one knows, he considers Cardinal Newman the best prose writer, but fights for, or rather is beaten for, the glory of Byron. His teacher happens to find an heretical thought in his composition. Amenable and untroubled, he corrects it and recants, without hesitation or regret.

Things change when the growing lad falls into mortal sin; we see him in a state of religious torment. Eternal damnation awaits him. For him the fountains of grace are dried up. But terror and pride prevent him from offering up to God one sole prayer at night, though he knows it is in God's power to take his life away while he sleeps and cast it into hell. Then come Father Arnall's sermons and the still increasing perturbation of the unhappy artist who hears in them a description of his own case. The vivid imagery which his sensibility provides makes the description of hell a thing of horror. Because his powers of analysis are already so great, no one knows as he does how to create his hell and to deserve it, too.

Then a long period of repentance and penance follows; and again the artist knows better than anyone else how to repent and do penance. Ambition always attends him. Everyone must know what a sinner he has been, and he never tires of performing acts of contrition. His life seemed to have drawn near to eternity; every thought of his, every instant of consciousness could be made to vibrate radiantly in heaven. And when his soul was enriched with spiritual knowledge he saw the whole world as forming one vast symmetrical expression of God's love and power. But he could not understand why it was in any way necessary that he should continue to live. I suspect that the artist could find no place for himself in that vast symmetrical expression. The artist cannot live side by side with others as their underling or equal.

The crisis soon presents itself. He is invited to enter the Society of Jesus. One expects enthusiastic acceptance. He is offered secret power and knowledge. It would seem that there was only one obstacle: the Jesuits are rather infantile in their literary tastes. They prefer Veuillot to Victor Hugo.

But then as he draws closer to that life devoid of passion or anxiety, an instinct stronger than piety arms him against consent. What would he do about that deep-seated shyness of his which prevented him from living under a stranger's roof? And how could he ever forget the pride that led him to regard himself as an exceptional being in every respect?

Everything turns on that refusal. Dedalus passes from

adolescence to manhood. Where now is the weak soul that shrank back from its destiny in order to turn aside and brood sorrowfully on the shame of its own wounds? Now he is alone, unprotected by anyone, happy, and close, very close, to the wild heart of life. As yet there seems to be no alienation from religion; except that the man of letters has quietly taken the place of the sinner, as calmly as a change of scene is carried out on a well-equipped stage. Walking amid the changing colours and sounds of his city, he remembers now the cloistered, silver-veined prose of Cardinal Newman, now the sombre humour of Guido Cavalcanti, to fall back in thought at last on Ibsen's message, or sing with Ben Jonson. If he is weary of the quest for beauty in the spectral words of Aristotle or Thomas Aquinas, he delights in the graceful songs of the Elizabethans. And his soul escapes the toils. 'My ancestors threw off their language . . . They allowed a handful of foreigners to subject them. This race and this country and this life produced me. I shall express myself as I am.' It almost seems as if the political and literary rebellion were more important than the religious one, and that he considers the break from religion less sharp because he still accepts the aesthetic theory of Aquinas. He goes from the most luminous faith to the rejection of it along an easy path which he enjoys. It will be part of the maturer Dedalus of *Ulysses* to remember that he had spent the greater part of his life in a sublime dream, and to suffer at the thought that humanity without faith can be considered nothing but a race of filthy animals. He will strive with himself to fill the dismal void left by faith. He will study modern philosophy, medicine, and natural sciences. In vain! His Catholic soul will tinge everything with its own colour, and the contradiction will be discordant, or (more rarely) will sing, but will never be stilled. And everybody says that in order to understand *Ulysses* one must be familiar with the teaching and practice of the Church. In fact the unbeliever Dedalus constantly makes use of the language believers taught him. He seems to be blaspheming; that is his destiny.

Ezra Pound has said that with *A Portrait of the Artist as a*

Young Man Gustave Flaubert finally makes his entry into English literature. He is accompanied by someone who is strongly in evidence – the author of *Ulysses*. If *Ulysses* did not exist it would be more difficult to discern how here in the *Portrait* Flaubert's limpid, impersonal narrative style is troubled by a new longing. Father Arnall's long sermon is probably the first attempt of Joyce as author to retire from the telling of the story after having introduced his character and entrusted him with the task. Nor, for other reasons, can one think of Flaubert when reading the love idyll in the *Portrait*. In its still unripe beauty and brevity it is the work of a poet who knows how to make a word do the work of a page and an image tell a story. One cannot forget that young girl, so poor in words, whose life is but a rosary of hours, strange as a bird's, gay at dawn, restless during the day, and tired at sunset; or perhaps, instead, that figure of the womanhood of Ireland (it is an Irishman who is speaking of his own country), a bat-like soul, awaking to the consciousness of itself in secrecy and loneliness, tarrying loveless and sinless with her mild lover, and leaving him to go and whisper her innocent transgressions into the latticed ear of a priest. Neither can one forget him, with his tragic vision of the lower life of his own ill-clad, ill-fed, dirty body. It makes him close his eyes in a spasm of despair and think, 'I must let her go her destined way and marry an athlete with a well-trained body which he washes every day.'

And now for *Ulysses*. One of those tiresome interviewers, the kind that thrives especially across the ocean, once asked Joyce, 'Why did you give your novel the title of Homer's epic poem?' Joyce replied, 'It is my way of working.' Joyce loves to fetter his imagination with chains. Joyce the fantast and rebel is a past master of discipline, a fantastic and rebellious discipline. As in Homer, this novel is divided into eighteen episodes, three of which form the Telemachiad, twelve the Odyssey, and three the Return of Ulysses. But these are chains that do not bind closely enough, and for Joyce they are not sufficient. I have seen a plan of this novel, put together by a French writer, Benoist Méchin, according to which each episode is said to be devoted to some part of the human body, and also to some art; and also regulated by a craft, and even suffused with a certain colour, so that the reader passing from one episode to another feels the narrator change mood in each of them. But not his individuality, for one sole line of a page of *Ulysses* would be enough to reveal the pen from which it came.

Larbaud informs us that Ulysses is the hero that Joyce loved and knew in his early youth, and that is the reason why in the period of his greatest creative power he dreamed of transplanting the cunning son of Laertes into our modern world. The work may first have been conceived as a parody. Today it stands by itself as a drama. In comparison the parody is lost. There remain certain points of contact accompanied by really Homeric laughter. Ulysses venerated the Gods and loved his family just as the Jew Bloom does, but he dwelt too long on the island of Circe and took a long time to return to the arms of his wife, just as Bloom does, who on his way home passes through the most disreputable quarter of the city. Many Homeric characters have their modern counterparts, but in a light which is humiliating to moderns. So it is with many episodes. The wind, Aeolus, is transformed into the Press. Without having any intention of defending the Press from outrage, I must own that in order to understand the author's intention one must refer back to the number of the episode. In others, however, the intention is evident. When Bloom is inflamed at the sight of Gerty MacDowell, we remember the episode of Nausicaa but we have no time to laugh. The perspicuity of certain cross-sections which show the whole physical and moral character of Bloom prevents that. Every episode might seem a separate story if they were not all rigorously held together by the unity of time (19 hours of the 16th of June 1904), and if in each of them there did not appear one of the two protagonists, Bloom or Stephen, who, as Larbaud says, are the two vehicles that carry us through the city, or to speak more precisely, through life. But there can be no doubt about it, the whole forms a real novel. Slight incidents bind the episodes together. A cloud in the sky is seen by Dedalus and eighty pages further on by Bloom, who does not appear till the fourth episode. Bloom is in mourning because he has to go that morning to the funeral of Dignam, and so everyone he meets talks to him about the dead man – whom we have not known and whom we shall never know – for now everyone likes him, a liking, however, which does not prevent them from turning him this way and that on their palms like a spurious coin. There is a woman who during those hours is about to become a mother, and she proves a well of knowledge and humour and philosophy for those who know her and are near her. An event which is evidently the most important one for Joyce, which holds the novel together, and which in the end we feel to be important for us, too, is the following. At the close of a memorable day the scholar Dedalus comes to the point of feeling the Jew Bloom to be a kind of father to him, while Bloom for his part, amid dreams and adventures, is also aware of a sense of fatherhood. The incident is plausible because Bloom has lost his son, and Stephen would like to find some substitute for his own living father, whose tenor of life is enough to explain Stephen's mood of despair. The approach is rendered possible by other reasons. The Jews and the Irish are both nations whose languages are dead. Stephen, moreover, is attracted by one who is very far from his own way of thinking, and feels a relief in communion with one who has never known all the culture that obsesses Stephen. One must allow that Stephen is less convinced of belonging to Bloom and never admits it explicitly, while Bloom proclaims his paternal affection and feels its duties and responsibilities. But such cases of affectionate fathers and indifferent sons often crop up. And one must confess, too, that when they talk together for a long time they discover that they agree only on one point and that a negative one: the lack of influence of gas-light or electric light on heliotropic trees. As this is often the tenor of the intellectual contacts between father and son, those between Stephen and Bloom are consequently legitimized. More important is the fact that there are some casual analogies between the notation of words of those languages.

Such in the plainest words is the picture. It is easier and
quite as important to speak of its frame. Here, the imper-
sonality of the author expresses itself by transforming novel
into drama. Many episodes are narrated by one character or
another, even if raffish or ignorant, and this invests certain
ingenuous creations which emerge from these discordant
tones with enormous importance. In other episodes the two
principal characters, Bloom and Stephen, communicate
directly with the reader, their solitary thoughts taking the
form of a monologue. They walk about with their brain-pans
uncovered. They say their say, and straightway without
further ado you are told their thoughts which colour or
discolour what they say, or deny it or flaunt it, or even forget
it. An important part of life passes through those two brain-
pans: the present broken up like light in a prism, the past
when it still aches or when it can be laughed at, or when like
lightning it flashes out of the darkness of night only to plunge
back into it again – learning and history in the brain-pan of
Dedalus, and in Bloom's, science and life as it strikes this
canvasser and constant reader of newspapers.

Listen to how Larbaud gives warning of the danger which
Joyce runs by cutting the author completely out of the story.
At first the reader is confused. He turns up in the middle of a
conversation that seems to him disconnected, between
people whom he does not at once distinguish, in a place that is
not described nor even mentioned. Such a book is not for the
careless reader; but we understand the density of content
which thought of this kind, that flashes and reveals itself in a
brief word, gives this long novel. The density is such that
when Dedalus thinks: 'History is a nightmare from which I
am trying to awake'; or again: 'To prolong all that they waste
monkey-glands', we suffer all the more because much of that
derided life is recorded in the book.

As an approach to this wonderful novel, I should like to
give you some of the results of Joyce's introspection into the
minds of the two principal characters. In the case of Stephen

it is astonishing. In the first episode we learn that he refused to kneel down at the bedside of his dying mother. A friend says to him: 'The aunt thinks you killed your mother . . . You could have knelt down . . . There is something sinister in you . . . you have the cursed jesuit strain in you, only it's injected the wrong way.' Not a word from Dedalus reveals that he feels any remorse.

He walks the streets of Dublin proudly, ashplant in hand, a notorious unbeliever, the self-ironizing superman, with decaying teeth and no money for the dentist. Yet when he can stand aloof even at the very moment when he is conversing with others, he is at once in the presence of his mother's ghost. Soon after her death she appeared to him, her body already half-wasted, the eyesockets empty, in the loose grave-clothes she wore in her coffin, and he could smell the odour of wax and rosewood of the death chamber. She bent upon him, mute and reproachful, surrounded by a choir of virgins and angels, singing in Latin the praises of the Mother of God. She turned now to heaven to pray for him, now to him to urge him to pray. She has become his constant companion. He defends himself: 'There, mother, let me live my own life.' Sometimes he would like to exorcize her. The ghost is there, but perhaps it is some devil that has taken the form of his mother. When, in some episodes, Dedalus seems to draw apart from us, the author, in order to describe the nature of his loneliness, quotes by way of explanation the Latin words sung by the choir.

In the episode which it has now become conventional to call the Walpurgisnacht, Stephen is drunk and his relations with his mother quicken to new intensity. In his intoxication he thinks he can assuage his anguish and at length gives it utterance: 'They say I killed you, mother . . . Cancer did it, not I. Destiny.' But the mother answers reproachfully: 'Who saved you the night you jumped into the train at Dalkey with Paddy Lee? Who had pity for you when you were sad among the strangers? Prayer is allpowerful. Prayer for the suffering souls in the Ursuline manual . . .' Stephen shouts abuse at her, and she becomes gentler: 'Tell the servant to make you

every night that boiled rice that was so good for you when you
were tired after your brain work. Years and years I loved you,
O my son, my firstborn . . .' Stephen himself, who imagines
these things, is shaken by the vividness of his memories. If it
is a ghost, it is his mother's. However, he protests in French,
in English, in Latin as if to show off his learning. It is tragic to
be an unbeliever when there are still saints in heaven, even
though they be transmuted into aesthetes, and when our
circumambient air is peopled with ghosts. Often when there
is no ghost, in its place there is a thought, which is quite the
same thing. Here is Stephen standing beside a boy whom he
is teaching at school: 'Lean neck and tangled hair, and a stain
of ink, a snail's bed. Yet someone had loved him, borne him
in her arms and in her heart. But for her the race of the world
would have trampled him under foot, a squashed boneless
snail. She had loved his weak watery blood drained from her
own. Was that then real? The only true thing in life? . . . She
had saved him from being trampled under foot and had gone,
scarcely having been. A poor soul gone to heaven: and on a
heath beneath winking stars a fox, red reek of rapine in his
fur, with merciless bright eyes scraped in the earth, listened,
scraped up the earth, listened, scraped and scraped . . . Like
him was I. These sloping shoulders, this gracelessness. My
childhood bends beside me. Too far for me to lay a hand there
once or lightly. Mine is far and his secret as our eyes. Secrets,
silent, stony sit in the dark palaces of both our hearts: secrets
weary of their tyranny: tyrants willing to be dethroned.'

The poet, as much in drunkenness as in his unceasing
effort to delve in the earth which would willingly bury all
ancient images, finds distraction in quaint researches con-
cerning Shakespeare's life, which is nothing but a convenient
hunting ground for all unbalanced minds. But while he is
talking scornfully of the genius, this anguished thought
forms in his brain: 'Are you condemned to do this?' And
again, regarding so many theories, he turns to the Lord and
prays: 'I believe, O Lord, help my unbelief. That is, help me
to believe or help me to unbelieve!' Stephen is not yet able to
interdict his habit of prayer.

Bloom is the worthy companion of Stephen, and as whole and important as he. He has been compared to Falstaff, to Pickwick, even to Don Quixote. He has, I would say, greater freshness than Dedalus, who from the first to the second novel has developed from early youth to maturity, while Bloom, the protagonist of the poem, is here born whole in a single ecstasy. Joyce, as he would say himself, drew Dedalus forth from his pocket, while he had to go seek Bloom in the wide world. The cold detachment with which Dedalus is depicted changes in the portraiture of Bloom to cold cruelty. This has led to a suspicion of anti-Semitic bias in Joyce, which – if it really exists – does not seem to me to have succeeded in producing the desired result. We love the little Jew who delights us and arouses our compassion more than the scholarly and arrogant Dedalus. Herbert Gorman says that he follows him with his best wishes.

Bloom is a smiling personage, yet he bears a family likeness to the tragic Stephen, but with one of those odd variations in which Nature indulges. In both, the dream is stronger than reality, only that in Dedalus when it is not an obsession it is the intense activity of a philosopher and a poet. With Bloom the dream is a repose which he seeks and loves, and in which he is lulled as in sleep. With Stephen the dream adorns the life he lives and despises with elegant phrase and gorgeous imagery; with Bloom it takes the place of the life he longs for and will never know. And further, if we knew only what Dedalus says and not his inmost thoughts, we should know a part, though not the most important part, of his character; we should know nothing of Bloom, because hardly anything of him comes out into the air and sunlight. Bloom knows a lot. By dint of reading newspapers, a great many novelettes and second-rate novels, and by diligently repeating in his dreams what he has learnt, he knows as much of natural philosophy and the history of Ireland and of Israel as his memory has helped him to pick up. He even approaches Shakespeare, whom he knows to have been a great genius, and being a very practical man though given to dreaming, he looks into him for the solution of the difficult problems of practical life and of his dream-life as well. The answers he obtained did not convince him. He tried to square the circle, but he also deeply pondered the importance of the latest discoveries, and could feel their momentousness with a whole-hearted wonder that made them seem as new to him as if he himself had just at that instant made the discoveries. He longs for wealth and so can dream of it. There would not be time enough for him to realize all his plans that overlap one another with the rapidity of waves of light. And then he dreams on a large scale: to utilize the refuse existing in Ireland with its population of four millions. He is more practical when he expects fortune to come to him in the shape of a wire at 2.59 p.m. tipping him the winner of a race to be run at 3.08 p.m. He might even find an imperforate brown seven shilling stamp issued at Hamburg in 1866. He is a very precise dreamer because he knows where every article he possesses came from, the name of the supplier, his exact address, and the price he paid for it in pounds, shillings and pence.

Bloom is good-natured, and it costs him no effort to protect Dedalus, a task which he feels to be an honour. He has been baptized three times, but that does not save him, for when an angry citizen hears Bloom declaring that Jesus Christ was also a Jew he hurls a heavy pot at him, which would have killed him if it had hit him. Luckily the angry citizen represents Cyclops and is blinded by the sun.

This Ulysses is with Circe all the time. He also needs Platonic love and carries on an amorous correspondence with an unknown girl. From time to time his brain is perturbed by the fear that he has not hidden the letter containing a flower in his pocket well enough. A part of the fourth episode, in which we are introduced to Bloom, has been translated in the review *900*. He is there all of a piece, with that letter in his pocket and a friend who asks a favour of him and a handsome woman passing by who occupies his thoughts and becomes their main theme. In fact that woman reminds him of two others he saw passing the day before. He remembers them as if they were two important adventures, as he does everything that stimulates his dreams.

Everything Bloom thinks gets into his blood and affects it. For that reason I do not think it possible that he represents the scientist side by side with the poet Stephen. I cannot accept him as a scientist, and not because he asserts that Aristotle was taught by a rabbi whose name he cannot remember. He has created a world of his own, just as Stephen has. Being Stephen's father, he, too, may be allowed to be a poet.

This is confirmed in my opinion by what happens in the episode which forms the crisis, perhaps the purpose of *Ulysses*, the Walpurgisnacht, as various critics have called it for its close resemblance with the scene of that name in *Faust*. Stephen and Bloom, both dead drunk, meet in a brothel. The images which obsess both and which are a reproduction of the day's adventures and a comment on them take body and are converted into aggressive living phantoms. In this fantastic way the squalid reality of the brothel rises like some unclean island from the mysterious sea. Bloom is evidently the less drunk of the two, for he is the first to sober up. But, the plaything of alcohol, he is like a ball in the hands of a wanton child. Not only does he argue with the phantoms he evokes but in the end he himself undergoes strange metamorphoses. He sees himself elected Lord Mayor of Dublin, hailed by bishops and rabbis. Parnell's brother proclaims him the successor of the uncrowned king. He is tried and condemned to death. He is transformed into Beaconsfield, Moses, Kossuth, Moses Maimonides, Robinson Crusoe, Moses Mendelssohn, Sherlock Holmes, Rothschild and Pasteur. If you know them both, you will not be surprised that of the two Stephen holds out better. It is he who becomes violent, but in the circumstances that is almost normal. Only once for an instant does he see himself transformed into Cardinal Stephen Dedalus, adorned with a rosary of corks. This too is a thing that might easily happen to him: a symbol of his has got drunk with him.

These, whom I have endeavoured to describe, are two of

the citizens who were going about Dublin on that day. But a part of the population may be said to have poured into the novel, and some have kept their real names. In fact, people say that when the novel began to be spoken of in Dublin, the inhabitants of that city were divided into two factions: those who wished and those who feared to be in it.

Just as the wrath of Citizen Joyce reminds me of that of a certain Tuscan, so his resolute diligence in ransacking his native town in order to find material for his novel reminds me of some of our writers. Will commentators rise up and tell us whether those Fuccis, Argentis and Schicchis lived at such and such an address and actually behaved so?

I am not a critic, and when I read these notes over again I doubt whether I have given a clear idea of this novel. It seems to me insufficient praise of it to say that it is the most representative novel that has appeared in the early part of our century. It was not in my mind to settle what place in the world of letters should be assigned to Joyce's work nor trace the relationship with what has preceded it. Like any simple-minded reader, I have just tried to get you to share my admiration for it.

One critical observation I can make, and that is suggested by a good memory and not by any critical sense. It is this: that I can prove that Sigmund Freud's theories did not reach Joyce in time to guide him when he was planning his work. This statement will astonish those who discover in Stephen Dedalus so many traits that seem beyond doubt to have been suggested by the science of psychoanalysis: his narcissism which will probably be attributed not to his being an artist but to his being a first-born son, the adored mother who changes into a haunting spectre, the father despised and shunned, the brother forgotten in a corner like an umbrella, and finally the eternal struggle in him between his conscience and his subconscious.

There is something more. Might not Joyce have borrowed from psychoanalysis the idea of communicating the thoughts of his characters at the very moment in which they are formed in the disorder of a mind free from all control? On this head the contribution of psychoanalysis can be ruled out, for Joyce himself has told us from whom he learnt this technique. In fact, his words were enough to confer celebrity on the venerable Edouard Dujardin, who had used this technique thirty years earlier in his *Les Lauriers sont coupés*.

For the rest I can bear good witness. In 1915 when Joyce left us he knew nothing about psychoanalysis. Moreover, his knowledge of current German was too weak. He could read some poets, not scientists. Yet at that time all his works, including *Ulysses*, had already been conceived.

From Trieste he went to Zürich, the second capital of psychoanalysis. Undoubtedly he became acquainted there with the new science, and there is reason to think that for a while he more or less believed in it. But I never had the satisfaction of knowing him to be a psychoanalyst. I left him ignorant of psychoanalysis. I found him again in 1919 in open revolt against it – one of those scornful rebellions of his by which he shook himself free of everything that hampered his thought. 'Psychoanalysis?' said he to me: 'Well, if we need it, let us keep to confession.' I was dumbfounded. It was the rebellion of the Catholic in him, enhanced with greater harshness by the unbeliever.

Joyce's works, therefore, cannot be considered a triumph of psychoanalysis, but I am convinced that they can be the subject of its study. They are nothing but a piece of life, of great importance just because it has been brought to light not deformed by any pedantic science but vigorously hewn with quickening inspiration. And it is my hope that some thoroughly competent psychoanalyst may arise to give us a study of his books, which are life itself – a life rich and heartfelt, and recorded with the naturalness of one who has lived and suffered what he writes. They are far worthier of study than that poor *Gradiva* of Jensen's, which Freud himself honoured with his celebrated comments.[1]

1. 'Delusions and Dreams in Jensen's *Gradiva*', published in 1907 [J.G-R.]

INDEX

This index omits members of the Veneziani and Schmitz families mentioned only in passing, and does not include the Appendix.